Rewrite Your Story

Kay Fabella

The Story Finder

DEDICATION

For my sister, Kara. This book started as a series of love letters to you as I watched you step into the new chapter of *your* story. I wouldn't have done this without your constant support from afar. I'm so proud of you, Ading, and I love you always.

-Your Ate

CONTENTS

SECTION 3: REWRITE

INTRODUCTION

Back in 2009, on a sunny Saturday morning in Boston, I reached for the phone to call my parents in California, "Mom, Dad... I've been crying for four hours straight. I can't stop it. I have no idea why I'm sad. What's wrong with me?"

It was the beginning of a year-long battle with clinical depression. I realized the pace at which I'd been working for so long was no longer sustainable. I was 22 years old.

My entire trajectory up until that point had been defined by high achievement. I was considered a gifted child and started reading at age two. I was studying algebra by age ten, graduated from high school at 16, and college at 19. I finished two university degrees in three years and I was at my first job out of college at a highly prestigious institution.

I was coasting on a sea of limitless potential and towards what I thought was a promising, successful future. I was bright-eyed, open and eager to learn from my new bosses and colleagues.

But I'd never learned the importance of limits and boundaries. I'd never learned to be anything less than "all in" on whatever was in front of me. I'd never learned to question whether or not there was a purpose to the work I was assigned to do — I just believed in the promise of me getting closer to "success" which was defined as job stability, financial security, a Master's degree, and enough to afford a mortgage and settle down. I didn't question it (why did I need to?) because this definition I'd been taught to accept my whole life made sense.

So, I happily volunteered for extra projects and weekend hours at the expense of my social life, sleep, and any semblance of balance outside of the office. I wore busy like a badge of honor and patted myself on the back for all-nighters I pulled alongside other co-workers. I convinced myself it was all worth it. Work was all I knew and as far as I was concerned, anything else was just a distraction.

Until one day work burned me out to the point it almost killed me.

Depression is the worst thing that can happen to a high achiever. It comes out of nowhere when you least expect it. You feel empty and heavy, exhausted and overwhelmed, disoriented and confused. So naturally, you try to control it, diagnose it, and rationalize it. And when trying to think your way out of it doesn't work, you start to ask yourself the important questions.

How did I get here? Was this what success was supposed to look like? Was this the life I even wanted to begin with? I was working anywhere from twelve to sixteen hours a day, six to seven days a week, trying to move my way up the ladder for a payoff I was no longer sure I even wanted. And for what? For someone else's definition of success? Or my own?

This was my wake-up call.

It took me a year to trust my own mind and feel like I was myself again. Looking back, I realized I'd spent so much time caring about proving that I *could* be successful that I'd never stopped to ask myself what my idea of success *actually* looked like.

I realized my definition involved joy, well-being, freedom, love, adventure, fulfillment, wonder and purpose.

For the first time in my life, I tuned out the noise of what I thought others expected of me and tuned into what my heart truly desired. I started to adopt practices to take better care of myself — away from meds and hospitals. By prioritizing self-care, redefining what success looked like for me, and learning to be willing to start over, I started to rewrite my story.

For every life decision, the only question I asked myself was, "What feels like the next right thing for *me*?"

I decided to take a chance and move back to Spain where I'd studied for a semester in college. I'd fallen in love with the country and culture and felt called to return. I planned to move abroad, finally become fluent in Spanish, earn money teaching English, and explore Europe while figuring out my next steps.

Nine years, a Spanish husband, and five years in business later, I now call Madrid home.

Today, I'm an expatpreneur running a bilingual business in English and Spanish from my home base of Madrid, Spain. I now get to help companies — whether they're solopreneurs, start-ups or Fortune 500s — share their stories effectively to attract and connect with the customers that matter to them. I'm especially passionate about helping underrepresented business owners increase their visibility to grow their audiences online.

You see, I've had a lifelong fascination with storytelling. I'd often indulge in Harry Potter, Lord of the Rings, or geek out on the latest sci-fi movie. But it wasn't until I was seven years old that I realized the power of stories to affect change on a personal level.

Growing up with, let's say, a "non-European-looking face", you realize quickly that you'll always get asked, "Where are you from?"

And then the inevitable second question, "No, where you are *really* from?"

At first, it used to frustrate me. After all, as a kid, all you want is to blend in, not be reminded of how you're different.

But eventually, I started to see the "second question" as an opportunity to unclench my fists and open my hands to engage with them. I could tell them that I was the daughter of Filipino immigrants who moved to the US for a better life for themselves and for their kids. I could tell them that I was, in fact, *really* from Los Angeles. In this way, I honored my heritage while helping someone expand their view of the world - all by telling them my story.

That lesson of the power of stories to connect human beings and change perceptions never left me. When it came time to start my business, I realized the very same skill I'd been developing my whole life – storytelling – was exactly what many brands were struggling to communicate with their audiences.

So in 2014, I began operating full-time as a brand storyteller and visibility strategist.

My life couldn't be further from where I was (literally and figuratively!) ten years ago. And it's because I took the time to understand what made my soul feel alive, decided to pursue it, and created it for myself. I went from scared and settling for a lackluster life based on what I thought was expected of me to building a life on my terms. Now any success I achieve, big or small, is celebrated because it came from what I wanted.

I'm assuming if you're reading this book you're not in love with your life right now and you're looking for ways to change it. Or maybe things look like they're going great on paper but you still feel unfulfilled deep down.

You don't have to pick up your life, move to another country, fall in love with a handsome Spaniard, and start a business in another language. But you do have to decide to go from *wishing* you could create a life you love to *taking action* to create a life you love.

You'll probably have to do things you can't imagine doing right now. You'll have to redefine success and happiness for yourself 100% on your own terms. You'll have to dust off dreams your eight-year-old self tucked away in a box somewhere that your twenty-eight-year-old self said were too crazy, too risky, or too outlandish to ever come true. You'll have to start believing in things before they're possible. You'll have to check in with yourself regularly to make sure your head, heart, and gut are all aligned unanimously around your decision. You'll have to push past your fears and existing beliefs about yourself and get comfortable doing things that may make you feel really uncomfortable.

…I didn't say change was easy.

But here's the alternative: waking up in the middle of the night realizing your life is speeding past like a runaway car and you're not the one in the driver's seat.

Now tell me, which one is more terrifying?

You don't have to reach rock-bottom as I did. You can decide today to make a change. You can decide that today is the day that you pick up the pen, turn to a crisp new page, and start writing the next chapter in your story.

One day? Or Day One? The choice is yours, my friend.

MY STORY

Confession: I didn't know what I wanted to be when I grew up. I wasn't one of those people you see in movies who just knew they were destined to be a marine biologist or a writer.

I was really good at singing. But I was told growing up that singing wasn't a lucrative career, so that was out. For a while, I thought I wanted to be a doctor like my dad. Eventually, I learned to turn my indecision into a funny answer to my Titas' questions at family parties.

(Side note #1: if you're Filipino, all adult figures are considered extended family. We don't refer to family friends as "Mr" and "Mrs" but rather "Tito" (uncle) and "Tita" (aunt), which can get quite confusing when you're asked how many family members you actually have.)

"What do you want to be when you grow up, Kay?" they would say as they bent down to speak to me, "You must want to be a doctor like your dad, huh?"

(Side note #2: if you are Filipino, you know what this Tita voice sounds like when they get to the "huh" at the end – it's more of a "haaaaaah".)

To which I'd reply, "Well... yes... but I'd like to be a singing doctor. I'll see patients during the day and sing at night!"

They'd laugh and ask, "But when would you sleep?" To which I'd shrug and they'd laugh some more and then turn back to their real grown-up conversations.

Honestly? The only thing I really wanted to be when I grew up was free. Free to do whatever I wanted, when I wanted, wherever I wanted.

The problem was that "free" wasn't a career option. It was something you were supposed to grow out of when you became an adult. So, I crossed my fingers and hoped the answers would be revealed to me as I got older. But I never got that tingle of passion when I thought about my future life and career.

As I got older, the indecision got worse. I went from school to school, eventually splitting my high school years between a local public high school as a freshman and a rural Massachusetts preparatory school from sophomore to senior year. Any dreams of a Dead Poets Society professor to guide me through my three years in boarding school were quickly chucked out the window. Everyone was smarter, more verbose at sharing their insights on command, surer of themselves, even faster than I was. It was jarring to go from star student to feeling invisible in classrooms with my professors.

To make matters worse, instead of giving me clarity on what I could do, I was told over and over what I *couldn't* do. A high school trigonometry teacher straight up told my parents I just didn't have the brain for math (ironic considering I'd studied algebra at age ten). I got less-than-stellar grades in biology, physics, and chemistry (so the doctor option was off the table). The sports I loved growing up as a kid like swimming, basketball, and tennis were out of reach because teammates were all faster, taller and stronger than me (so that star athlete scholarship was a no go, if it was ever even an option). Heck, I wasn't even the best singer in my class anymore, relegated to backup roles in the choir or in the high school musical (so singing professionally felt like it was ruled out, too).

I started to panic. At 16, I was "running out of time" to "figure out my life" and what I stood out in so I could apply for college… and I kept coming up empty. I felt like my options for a successful future and career were dwindling before I even graduated.

I was desperate to explore the world before college because I knew, deep down, it would help me find myself. But that was the exact opposite of what my hard-working immigrant parents — who'd just spent a small fortune making sure I had the chance to attend a rigorous school they'd only dreamed of growing up in the Philippines — wanted for me.

So, when I got accepted to college, I made a promise to myself that I would finish in three years' time. Both to save my parents from having to pay for my sister and I attending college simultaneously and to get out and explore the world as quickly as possible.

When I got there, I kept hoping that I'd have an amazing professor like I'd read about in books and seen movies; someone who took an interest in me and mentored me. Or that I'd find a life-changing class that would illuminate my path forward in life. Luckily, I found one in a Global Public Health class which led to my immediate post-college career path. It wasn't my passion, but it was a sign. I followed it and ran with it as long as I could before it was time to let go... and you know that story ended.

What I've realized is this… there are some people who have an internal resolve, who know what they're destined to do. They're single-minded in their focus and solid in who they are. Nothing can shake them or distract them from the path they know they're meant to take. I've always envied those people. But the more I speak to other successful leaders and business owners, the more I realize those people are in the minority.

The rest of us are destined to shine, but we can't see that we're capable of doing so without the help of others. We need wisdom. We need guidance. We need to make our own decisions but with the safety net of acceptance if we fail. We need constant encouragement until we feel like we can stand on our own two feet.

I think back to every single person in my youth who told me in not so many words that I wasn't good enough. My heart breaks for my younger self because she was too insecure to trust who she was and what she wanted, so she believed them.

It took me starting a business to learn to take charge of my story and become the author of my own life. I finally allowed myself to be who I was and surrounded myself with others who accepted me. I felt like I belonged because I had others in my life who truly saw me and encouraged me to shine. And one by one, the stories I told myself — they all started to change.

So now I want to ask you...

What stories are you telling yourself? Stories about what you can and can't achieve. What is and isn't possible. What you are and aren't capable of. What you can and can't change. Write them all down and *flip the script*.

That teacher who told me I don't have a brain for math? I now use math every day as I measure the numbers in my business.

And that's just one example of how I've let go of old stories and created new ones.

Your story can always change.

Your fingers are on the keyboard.

Your pen is on your blank page.

It starts with writing a new word, a new sentence, a new paragraph and eventually a new chapter.

Here's to the new stories we'll tell ourselves and to the new stories we'll write.

SECTION 1

RECOVER

CHAPTER 1

WHY YOU'RE STILL PLAYING SMALL

"Do the best you can until you know better. Then when you know better, do better."

-Maya Angelou

Writing this book has been an all-encompassing exercise in personal development. I'm probably not supposed to tell you this as someone who looks like she "has her shit together". But like Outkast, I'm... I'm... just being honest!

I started writing this book absolutely inspired, motivated by the idea to take everything I've learned to live a successful life on my terms and share it with you. I know the message I'm ready to share is going to help you get out of your own way, own your awesome and step into the success story we both know you're meant to live. I'm assured by clients and friends that I'm bright, thoughtful, articulate and a fantastic teacher, that this book is a long time coming and that my story needs to be told.

But every day I sat down to write it from a completely different state of mind. I questioned whether I was supposed to be sharing this with you in the first place. I struggled with defining what success means for me and felt like a fraud for trying to give answers when I haven't "figured it all out" yet myself. I wondered if this book would actually make a difference or if it would just add to the noise and disappear into the void. I laughed at myself for thinking I could even be an author to begin with.

Every day, heck, every minute I decided to write another chapter of this book was a hard-fought miracle, a small victory in the ongoing battle of self-perception being waged inside my mind.

I would get a glimpse of you, the reader I have never met, and I would swell with pride at the thought of this book in your hands… immediately followed by the fear that you'll never bother to read it.

I was assaulted with old stories my mind pulled up from its archives that showed me I'm not good enough, sufficient enough or capable enough to write this book.

And one by one, I had to actively negate those outdated stories and remind myself what and who I am now. I had to consistently decide that in spite of myself, I get to decide to refocus my energy into doing instead of getting caught up in my fear.

I'm telling you this to show you the battle against yourself, against your fears and insecurities, against your own ego, screaming to protect you from anything outside of your comfort zone… it doesn't go away.

There is no magic bullet. There is no Nirvana that keeps you in a state of enlightenment and endless prosperity once you decide to take charge of your life. In fact, the further you go towards the success you desire, the more challenging this internal battle will become.

But it's up to you to choose to believe you can and push forward anyway.

Think of how much time you spend on any given day hating on yourself instead of *believing* in yourself. You tell yourself you're lazy, incapable, unworthy, but to what end? Wouldn't you be closer to the life you truly desired if you chose, instead, to look for confirmation that you're brilliant? That you're capable of anything? That you're magnificent and infinite? And then, from that state of mind, decided to make your dream life happen?

It takes the same amount of energy... so why is drama our default?

We invest all our time and energy in believing that we're not good enough because we've been taught to stop loving who we are. We've gotten so used to our negative knee-jerk reactions to ourselves that we never think to question them or ask where they come from. We assume that the thoughts that run through our heads that beat us up on the daily are true and accept them as our truth.

But once we become aware of the thought patterns and behaviors that are holding us back we can actively work to change them and, in the process, set ourselves free to pursue our dreams and deepest desires.

It all starts with loving ourselves more.

So let's run your very own self-love audit, shall we?

- What's the first thing you think when you look in a mirror?
- What do you think when someone you know succeeds at something you'd love to do, but have been too terrified to try for yourself?
- What goes through your head when you see someone drive past you in a luxury car?
- What happens inside you when you try your best and you fail?
- Or when a friend lets you down?
- Or when someone criticizes you?
- Or when you trip over your own two feet for the umpteenth time while racing to catch the bus?
- Or when you find yourself near a group of people who look successful?
- Or when you lose your temper and snap at someone who didn't deserve how you lashed out at them?

In each one of these instances, are you speaking to yourself from a place of love or a place of loathing? Notice how you speak to yourself and challenge yourself to replace that automatic message with something far less... nasty.

For example, if the first thing you think when you look in a mirror is to fixate on flaws like "my lips are too thin" or "my forehead is the size of Saturn," try to replace it by focusing on the features you do like.

Or if the first thing you think when your friend lets you down or your significant other dumps you is "I always attract the wrong people into my life" or "ugh, another confirmation that I'm unlovable," try to replace it with "I must not have communicated what I needed so I'll do better next time" or "I'm worthy of love and now there is space for someone who can give that to me."

You have to break free and release yourself from the idea that this current version of you is who you'll always be.

Now, you may be thinking, "Well that's easy for you to say, Kay, because you've got it all figured out living that fabulous life of yours in Spain." But I'm just as guilty as you are of sliding back into negative self-talk. (The beginning of this chapter proves that!)

But every day I decide to move forward in spite of the daily onslaught of less-than-loving thoughts. The only difference between you and me is that I decide not to accept thoughts that could keep me stuck, and instead work to actively cultivate kindness towards myself.

Trust me, the time you're wasting on loathing the size of your nose is detracting from every minute you could be spending finding that dream career… finding the cure for cancer... ending poverty... or just making space for the family you've always wanted.

Yes, we are human. Yes, we feel emotions and we want to protect ourselves from past hurts. Yes, our comfort zones are much safer than venturing out into the unknown. Yes, it's easier to blame other people for our problems than it is to take responsibility for our own lives. But if you wanted to stay in your current status quo, you wouldn't be reading this book.

We are all capable of limitless possibilities with power beyond our wildest dreams... and most of us aren't using a fraction of it.

So, if you want to learn to kick your old friends Fear and Doubt out of the driver's seat, you need to start reprogramming the thoughts that go into your mind. Consciously and subconsciously. Which is exactly what we'll cover in the next chapter.

CHAPTER 2

WHAT'S HOLDING YOU BACK?

"Nothing around us is going to change until we have the courage to go deep inside, explore the demons that lie within, and eventually let them go."

-Gabrielle Bernstein

There is no one global definition of success that applies to everyone.

Even if you grow up in the US where everyone is striving to live out the "American Dream," success is going to be different depending on your circumstances. If you're an immigrant like my parents, your American Dream is to create a better life for your family that you wouldn't have had in your home country.

If you're born in the US, maybe success includes things like having a good-paying job, a spouse and kids, a house, a car and the ability to travel whenever you want. The options are even more undefined when you become an entrepreneur or business owner — there is no limit to what success looks like for you.

It's not always easy to define success, let alone know what it will feel like when you've achieved it. What are the steps you should take on your journey toward your definition of success? How do you know if you're on the right path to begin with?

For our entire lives, we've been conditioned to believe we are supposed to "grow up", land a job that makes a ton of money, get married, have kids, buy a house and take lots of vacations. That work isn't *supposed* to be fun. That growing up is *supposed* to be challenging. That if we do anything else outside of that, we might as well have chosen failure. And that "success" is based on being everyone else's (parents, siblings, teachers, friends, strangers) definition of what's "good" for us.

Until one day you decide to question whether those definitions of "good" or "success" are what you even wanted to begin with. The problem is, you've been conditioned for so long to believe what you're "supposed" to be, you naturally feel resistance. So when you decide to do something outside the norm, to even dare to dabble in the idea of something different, you find you're holding yourself back. Or you feel held back by others around you who've come to expect you to be or act a certain way. No wonder you feel stuck and frustrated!

But I'm gonna let you off the hook (just this once!) because it's not entirely your fault that you're this screwed up. It is most definitely your fault if you stay screwed up, but the foundation for your screwed-up-ness has been passed down to you from generations before in the form of patterns of behavior and an inherited belief system. Like putting your family reputation before your own happiness. Or a tendency to people-please instead of creating conflict. Or thinking that money is inherently dirty or evil. Or that pursuing your passion is a one-way ticket to Broke Town.

None of that started with you. In fact, most people are walking through life like they're in the Matrix, inside an elaborate illusion based on all the false messages they've been taught to accept as the truth.

But we sure as heck didn't start out that way. From the moment we enter this world, we are blank slates. We have no idea how things should or shouldn't be, what *we* should or shouldn't be. Because when we're born we just… are. We're sponges, absorbing and doing our best to process the information that's being thrown our way and trying to make sense of it.

As you grew up and became capable of interacting with the world around you, you started to receive stories from people about how things work. Your parents, teachers, all the people who raised you, supported by society at large, collectively imparted their beliefs onto you. Everything from what's considered an acceptable career, what kind of love you should look for, how much money you should earn, what body type is considered beautiful, what clothing is inappropriate, what university you should aspire to... it was all shared with you. And being the trusting, moldable mind that you were, you took it all in without question and believed these stories.

But unsurprisingly, the things they taught you weren't always true for you. In fact, in most cases, the messages you received from wise, well-meaning adults who wanted to love, guide and protect you were passed down from their parents, and their parents, and their parents before them. Stories they accepted as true, regardless of whether or not they actually were.

All of those beliefs you inherited on how to be, do or act, and what "success" is and should look like... none of them are even accurate reflections of the beliefs of who you heard it from to begin with. It's like an ongoing chain of whispers that are passed down for centuries, collectively crippling us instead of lifting us up.

And the messages handed down to you are affecting you even when you're not aware of it. How, you ask?

As human beings, we all have a conscious mind and a subconscious mind. Most of us only know about our conscious mind because that's where we process information. But here's the lowdown on how our brains actually operate and how we can use it to our advantage...

Our conscious mind is where we analyze everything we learn. Where we judge ourselves and others. Where we try to uncover all the potential places we could have lost our car keys. It's where we make mental notes of the next book to read or the next item to add to our grocery list. Or we decide that we're quitting sugar or committing to learning a foreign language or finally making use of our gym membership… you get the idea.

All of that happens inside our conscious mind, which fully develops sometime around puberty. It contains all of the thoughts, memories, and wishes that we're aware of at any given moment.

Our subconscious mind, on the other hand, is home to all the things we can't analyze; our feelings, instincts, and emotions. When we arrive on this planet as screaming bundles of joy, our subconscious is already fully developed. It believes everything and accepts it as the truth because it has no filter, no way of distinguishing between right or wrong, no way to rationalize with logic. And it's where we start housing our first tidbits of information we receive from the outside world. What our subconscious receives, retains and stores lays the foundation for who we are and how we move through life.

Think of your subconscious as if it were a tiny human. It doesn't know any better. It takes everything it's presented with at face value. Without the advice of a mature adult to guide it, the only way it knows to process information is based on what it receives. Your subconscious scans and absorbs what it learns from the people around you, starting with your family, your teachers and friends. Every tear, smile, tilted frown, furrowed brow, or hearty laugh was either confirmation that you should repeat a behavior or accept a belief, or reject it entirely.

Your subconscious took that data and stored it, laying the blueprint for your personality, your worldview, and for every decision you're predisposed to make. Most importantly, it's programmed to protect you from anything it perceives could cause you harm.

So the next time you're pulling your hair out and wondering what the hell your problem is — I promise, *it's not you*. It's because your subconscious mind is pulling the strings. It's why even with the best intentions we're baffled when the thing we envision for ourselves doesn't happen. It's why whenever you attempt to do anything new, try something different, or break a bad habit once and for all, you feel emotionally (and physically) uncomfortable. And it's why you're holding yourself back from living a successful life on your own terms.

Take, for instance, your belief system around money. Did you grow up in a household where money was a sore spot? Where your family lived from paycheck to paycheck and fought over every line item in their monthly budget? Where you had a parent you rarely saw because they were off trying to earn enough to send home? (Don't get me wrong. This doesn't mean you have a free pass to blame everything that's effed up about you on your parents. But more on that later.)

Whether or not you realized it, your subconscious absorbed these experiences without a filter and created a series of beliefs such as:

- Making money is a struggle.
- Money leads to problems in relationships.
- Men are the only ones who should make money in a household.
- It's because of money that I never saw my mom.
- Money = sacrifice = pain.

Fast forward to you as an adult. Consciously, you know you want to be making money effortlessly to live the lifestyle you've always wanted. But if your subconscious doesn't equate money with happiness, distrusts money and your ability to earn and keep it, or is somehow worried that your partner will be threatened if you earn more than they do… then it will do everything it can to keep money away from you.

If you have a subconscious belief that is working against you, you will always repel the thing you consciously say you want. So, what can we do to get our subconscious to work for us to succeed instead of against us, and rewrite our own story in the process?

1 - Become aware of what could be holding you back

Do an audit of the areas of your life that could use some more lovin'. Your career, your relationships, your health, your self-confidence. Then start asking yourself what are some subconscious beliefs that might be creating that reality for you?

I used to think everyone had it figured out except for me. I'd focus on other people's highlight reels and compare them to my own experiences — a dangerous combination when you're feeling confused and lost post-burnout. It was easy to keep believing that everyone else's life was working out for them perfectly and something was wrong with me.

Go through each area and write down the first five things that come to mind. This could be a conversation you remember with a parent or sibling, a teacher that you looked up to, or a specific childhood experience. Write down the stories that you could be telling yourself around those key areas of your life you'd like to improve.

2 - Challenge each story and decide if it's true for you

Take that list of stories and ask yourself if they're based on love or fear. Ask yourself, are you really afraid of commitment? Are you really unworthy of success? Are you really incapable of being loved? Or are all those just stories you're telling yourself?

Go through each story one by one and ask, is this really true? Is this true for me now? And if not, what can I choose to replace it with?

Over time, I became good at recognizing when I fell into comparisonitis. As soon as I'd catch myself looking outward to those around me and inventing a story in my head about how I was "less than" they were, I'd gently turn inward. Through the practices I cover later in the book, I learned to shift from feeling like I was failing on someone else's timeline, to accepting what felt true for *me*. The more I tuned in and focused on my own experience, the more clarity I found on how I wanted to move forward.

3 - Decide which stories no longer serve you

Once you have your list of stories, you should have physical proof in front of you of what's been holding you back from the life you crave. Whether that's wanting to finally take charge of your health, to get more hours of sleep each night, to travel more, to be a better partner or to uplevel in your career, having these stories written out in front of you will help you get clear on where you've come from — and what's been holding you back.

Go through each of those stories one by one that you've marked as untrue. Forgive yourself. Forgive whoever else is involved. If you'd like, you can even write each story down on a Post-it and (safely!) burn it, douse the flames with water and wash your hands clean. Then choose to let it go.

4 - Be willing to forgive others

In this process, you'll find the cause of your fear stems from a specific experience or person. You'll start to uncover grudges that go back years and years. Yes, we can continue to hold onto blame or resentment... but in the end we're only hurting ourselves. So much so that even when good things happen to you, your subconscious programming will kick in with, "I don't really deserve this" or "this is good now, but it won't last". Which means you'll always hold yourself back instead of permitting yourself to move forward.

Rather than continuing the cycle of loathing and self-sabotage, challenge yourself to forgive. Forgive your parents for trying their best and falling short. Forgive that teacher who said you'd never amount to anything or that mean girl who body-shamed you or that stranger who shouted something sexist or racist to your face. You don't even have to have the conversation with them to let them know you're forgiving them, just choose to do so on your own.

5 - Be willing to forgive yourself

In every instance, above all, forgive yourself. Forgive so you can let go of those experiences that have been consuming space and energy. Holding onto that resentment and anger will always block you from living the life of your dreams.

6 - Rewrite your story

For each of those stories you let go of, write a new story in its place.

- Replace your lack of commitment story with, "I commit and follow through when I say I will."
- Replace your feelings of unworthiness with, "I'm worthy and deserving of success."
- Replace your fear of being unlovable with, "I'm enough, and people love me as I am."

Keep them somewhere you'll see them every day and move through the world confident that it's already true.

Later on in this book, I'll give you some tools to help dive deeper into your subconscious mind and start reprogramming your limiting beliefs, and learn what's holding you back from living the life you truly desire. But for now, practice learning to step aside, stay present where you are, and up your awareness of what's going on underneath.

7 - Love yourself

There's no use in beating yourself up for "not being far enough ahead" or "not having this figured out by now". The point is, you're here *now*. You're making an effort. You're showing up and ready to do the work to make a change.

Love yourself for the person you are and for who you are on your way to becoming.

CHAPTER 3

CHANGE YOUR DEFINITION OF SUCCESS

"Define success on your own terms, achieve it by your own rules, and build a life you're proud to live."

-Anne Sweeney

Who's the first person who comes to mind when you think "success"?

Picture one of your heroes. Someone you look up to. Someone who radiates confidence and charisma. Someone who makes success look effortless.

Got someone? Good.

Now list all the reasons you admire them. They're accomplished. They're capable. They're natural communicators. They're good-looking. They're pre-destined for greatness. They're obviously so much better than you could ever be, right?

No... no... no.

Stop putting your idols on a pedestal.

When you look at someone else's success, it means you believe they have something you don't. That by some divine combination of genes, alchemy, and magic, they've been able to accomplish the impossible while the rest of us look on in awe and wonder.

Somehow, we think we can't learn their skill, gain their experience, or access their secret. So we sit back complaining or comparing. It's easier for us to stay inside our comfort zone and keep telling ourselves that because we'll never have what they have, we shouldn't even try.

Whether it's your boss, a celebrity, a friend, your partner, or an influencer, putting people you consider "successful" on a pedestal is much different than admiring them. And here's where we have to be careful...

In order to place someone else above us, it means we're considering ourselves as *beneath* them. We hold people we put on pedestals to a higher standard than we hold ourselves or others. We see them as "more than" and "better than" us because society has deemed them successful. But you only see the aspects of them they want you to see. And while they may have achieved success, it only applies to certain areas of their lives and specific arenas where they're considered an expert.

In other areas of their lives they have their shortcomings, just like you and me. We don't see them 24/7 (even if they seem to be on every social media platform possible). We're not around to watch them when they slip up. Curse. Make mistakes. Trip over their own two feet. Let people down. Indulge more than they should. They're human, too, after all.

When you put someone "successful" on a pedestal, your tendency is to focus only on what you lack. Whether or not you realize it, this has a negative impact on your own sense of self-worth and self-esteem because you're ignoring your own gifts, talents, skills and natural abilities.

There's nothing wrong with having people you aspire to be like or look up to as your heroes. But there *is* a danger in idolizing them to the point where you'll always see yourself as "less than" they are.

Remember... every "someone" started as a "nobody". Every master was once a beginner. It's your job to follow their clues to understand how they succeeded.

Oh, and I've got news for you... that person that you consider a "success"?

You're seeing them today at their Chapter 20 or 200, but their Chapter one was not so different from yours. They were a rough draft, unrefined, imperfect and in progress. So rather than looking at the end result of what they've achieved, I'd like to invite you to think of their first steps instead.

You see, when that successful person you admire first started out, they were just like you.

Hopeful, but terrified. Driven, but overlooked. Excited, but unsure of where to start. And with consistent effort every... single... day... they got to where they are now. Did it mean they got to where they are today overnight? No. Did they conquer their own Impostor Syndrome for good once they got to this magical fairy tale land called success? Not a chance.

Wanna know the only difference between you and them?

In spite of their doubts and insecurities, successful people chose faith over fear more times than they didn't.

Here's your challenge…

Take the person you most admire and spend a couple of hours doing an investigative Google search. I mean, really dig. Go through old YouTube videos. Find early podcast interviews or (gasp!) cassette tapes (remember those?). Scroll their Instagram feed to the very bottom. Use the Wayback Machine to see what their website looked like in its very first iteration.

This isn't for you to laugh at their expense — it's for you to see how not so very different their beginnings were from where you are now. After going down the research rabbit hole, you'll start to get a clearer sense of how they built what they've built and the steps they took.

We still have more work to do to determine what it is you want before you start modeling them… and we'll get to that later on. This exercise is just to get you to see that, yes, that person is more outwardly successful than you are. But it's important for you to see them as someone to admire instead of giving yourself another excuse to put yourself down.

So rather than putting them on a pedestal, out of your reach, reframe it. Bring them back down to earth. Think that they're just a few steps ahead of you on the path rather than high above you on some unreachable Mount Everest peak.

If you keep moving forward down the path like they have, choosing faith in yourself over fear, success is within your reach.

CHAPTER 4

LET GO TO LET FLOW

"Let it gooooo… let it gooooo…"

-Elsa, Frozen

Someone once told me that cemeteries are the most expensive real estate on the planet. To which I blinked back with a deer-in-the-headlights look, taken aback by how morbid it sounded.

Finally, I breathed out, "Why?"

He responded, "Think of all of the unrealized hopes, dreams, and ideas that could have changed the world that most people are too scared to act on during their lifetimes. By playing small and holding themselves back from who they could have become, their dreams died with them. And it came at a cost to humanity."

…I still get shivers thinking of that conversation because I know it's true.

We're not put on this Earth to just pay the bills and die. No matter where you fall on the spiritual spectrum, we were put here for a reason. Think of the seemingly impossible string of micro-miracles that had to happen for you to even exist. How could you possibly let yourself be anything less than the fully-realized bundle of awesome that you are?

But as we established in Chapter two, we still have work to do to unravel old limiting beliefs and make your subconscious a powerful ally working on your behalf. Living the life you've always imagined requires you to uplevel beyond anything you've ever done or been before. And it starts with letting go of those stories that are no longer serving you.

1 - Let go of the story that success "has to" look a certain way

For many people, success is based on what they own; a fancy car, a big house, and a well-paying job. For others, success is measured by their relationships with their family and friends. And for others, success is about the difference they're making in the lives of others.

There is no one right definition of success. There is only *your* definition.

And unlike what most people may think, success is not a final destination. Success is a continuous process. There is never a point where you reach your limit or completely fulfill your potential. You can always improve and strive to do better. Which means your definition of success can still evolve over time… and that's completely OK.

2 - Let go of the story that you're not capable

It's easy for us to look back through our past and find confirmation that we're not capable. The times we gave up. The times we started something only to leave it behind. Or those times we started something only to fail miserably. We tell ourselves that even if we wanted to succeed with every fiber of our being, we'll never achieve success, no matter how hard we try. The belief that we're not capable is enough to keep us stuck.

Start by believing in yourself. Decide that you're worth betting on, trust that you can do what you set out to do, and then get to work. By making a series of conscious decisions to follow through on what you say you'll do, you'll prove to yourself that you're more than capable of whatever you set your sights on accomplishing.

3 - Let go of the story that you're not worthy of success

Too often we feel unworthy of success. Many of us tend to think we don't deserve good things and that somehow we "deserve" to suffer. Maybe you tell yourself you can't complete what you started, or you always mess things up no matter how bad you want it. When you look back on your past and contemplate where things went wrong in your life, you think the common factor is you. You sabotage yourself and you find it difficult to approach setbacks without seeing them as confirmation of how undeserving you are.

If you don't feel like you're worthy, you will always find a way to sabotage yourself from allowing success (whatever that word means to you).

So cut yourself some slack for "failing" to achieve all the expectations that others have placed on you. With the bar of achievement set unrealistically high by our society and our own self-imposed standards, you've trained yourself to beat yourself up every time you fall short. You've developed a knee-jerk reaction of self-loathing instead of self-love.

Once you understand what makes you feel undeserving or unworthy, learn to cultivate compassion and forgiveness for yourself. Celebrate what you have accomplished and use it to bolster you as you move forward.

4 - Let go of the story that things must be perfect

We're taught to aim for perfection and nothing less. Perfectionism in our society is discussed mostly in terms of looks, money, or status. Sometimes it's used when discussing things like intellect *("Look how young she was when she started to read!")*, generosity *("Wow, their family donates the most money to that foundation every year!")*, consideration for others *("Your son is so polite that we've given him the Student of the Week award!")* or ambition *("She grew her business to six figures in just six months!")*. This can lead to feelings of failure whenever those ideals are not met. It makes us question our worth when we fail to be perfect.

I'm what you'd call a "recovering perfectionist". When you're an entrepreneur, you learn pretty quickly that aiming for perfect is the kiss of death. When you're also a storyteller who writes words for clients, trying to emulate their voice, tone, and style of doing business, "perfect" goes out the window... fast.

When you commit to a life of success on your terms, the new path you'll be embarking on will be full of challenges. The last thing you want to do is have your desire for perfection slow you down, blocking you from new ideas, making you overly critical of yourself and stopping your forward movement.

Instead, embrace each moment as a learning opportunity on the path to growth.

Progress > perfection. Done > perfect.

5 - Let go of the story that your past = your future

News flash: the past version of you does *not* dictate who you can become.

Now, I'm not gonna pretend that all of us start in the same place in life. You may not have had access to resources others have. But you shouldn't feel held back based on where you've come from.

As a storyteller, I've listened to the personal stories of hundreds of entrepreneurs overcoming adversity to build successful businesses. So regardless of whether you had to overcome homelessness, anxiety, violence, a life-altering injury, feeling like an outcast, flunking out of school, heartbreak or loss... please know that I acknowledge the pain you went through. There is, however, an important point to be made for whether you choose to let that experience define you or *refine* you.

Remember, it's never the experience that creates the pain and adversity for us — it's how we choose to think about it.

Don't get stuck in regret or beating yourself up for your less-than-ideal past. Let it go however you see fit. Learn from it and take the opportunity to improve yourself where you can. Forgive yourself and others. Or use your past story as motivation for you to change your circumstances for good. The only thing you can control is how you act in this present moment. Then the next. Then the next.

6 - Let go of the story that you need a "magic bullet" to succeed

Each year, millions are spent on advertising campaigns designed to sell you a "magic bullet" solution to your problems. To sell you the ONE THING you need to lose weight, be happy, save time or become successful. The problem with the magic bullet is that there is no "one thing" that's going to give you the shortcut from where you are to where you want to be.

But if you've learned anything from studying your heroes in Chapter three it's that there are no "secrets" or "shortcuts". There's only systematic hard work, cultivating strong habits and discipline, and choosing to believe in yourself more often than you don't.

Instead of looking for a magic bullet solution, do an honest assessment of your strengths and weaknesses. Imagine what the most ideal version of yourself looks like and determine what steps you'll need to become that person. Decide what you can improve upon and what habits you need to develop if you want to achieve success on your terms.

You and you alone know what's holding you back. Work to change one habit at a time or improve on one aspect of yourself at a time. Invest in resources like books or mentors where necessary. Once you've developed that habit, move onto the next one.

7 - Let go of the story that you need to be liked

Often when we decide to level up in our lives, we run into resistance from friends, partners, and family members. They've come to know us a certain way and this "new" upgraded version of who we are working to become may make them feel surprised at best; threatened at worst.

No matter how painful it is, stop trying to be liked. While it's very normal and human to want to feel needed, understood, accepted, liked, and loved, it's important to take a stand for who you are. You're making a decision to live a life aligned with your core values, passions, and talents. What could be more beautiful than that?

People will find a reason to dislike you no matter what you do, how pure your motives are, or how wonderful this new journey is for you. When this happens, chances are it's more about their issues and how your decision to improve your life will force them to question their own.

Instead of investing emotional energy in what you can't change, focus on the *why* behind your decision to bet on your success. Communicate with those who will support you unconditionally on your journey. Either choose to ignore the people who will try to hold you back or be willing to let them go.

8 - Let go of the story that you aren't worthy of love

Our value as human beings is inherent, not acquired.

Love yourself for the person you were, for the person you are, and for the person you are on your way to becoming.

Even before you begin your journey towards living the life of your dreams… or when you stumble along the way… or when you achieve the wildest goal you set for yourself… remember this:

You are worthy.

You are enough.

You are loved.

CHAPTER 5

THE MOST POWERFUL "F" WORD

"Holding onto resentment is like drinking poison and expecting the other person to die."

-Unknown

...that got your attention, didn't it?

If you only learn one thing from this book, I hope it's this: forgiveness.

It's the most powerful tool we have at our disposal because it sets us free. It helps us to unchain ourselves from blame, shame, and resentment and allows us to fully step forward as we truly are. Forgiveness is the reason I've been able to move beyond my shortcomings and past hurts to rewrite my story and consciously create my life.

In my teens and early twenties, I spent more time than I should have blaming everyone and everything for my problems. I resented people who looked happy, who seemed like they had it all together, and who appeared to move through life effortlessly — obviously they had it better than I did and *that's* why they're so happy, I'd think to myself as I'd eyeroll. #SnarkMasterFlex

But I'll never forget a conversation I had at my first job with a senior colleague. I was hosting a housewarming at my first apartment as a working professional (adulting, FTW!). It was an intimate gathering and we settled ourselves around the fondue I'd set up for us. At one point, the group conversation broke off into one-on-ones and my colleague turned to me.

He said, "So Kay, you're fresh out of university then, right?"

"Yes," I replied, expecting him to follow up with something along the lines of asking me what degree I had studied or what my career goals were.

Instead, he said, "Have you forgiven your parents yet?"

Talk about social quicksand! The question took me completely by surprise and I didn't have enough time to process. I sheepishly grinned, half-laughed, passed it off as a joke and changed the subject.

That night, it got me thinking about whether there was truth to his question. And it's a question that still stirs up feelings more than a decade later.

I realized it wasn't just my parents I had to forgive for whatever I was unfairly blaming them for. Sometimes I'd recount old conversations with friends I'd fought with and lost. Or I'd get myself worked up whenever I remembered times random strangers passed judgment and assigned me a narrow racial identity based on how I looked.

I wasn't doing myself any favors by replaying tired reruns in my head of who'd hurt me and how. Which meant I had two choices: I could continue to blame others, stay angry, and beat myself for letting it happen. Or I could decide to let it go.

Now, don't get me wrong, choosing to forgive someone does not make you a doormat. It does not justify or condone bad behavior. You may have been on the receiving end of treatment that is downright unforgivable. But how does it serve you to carry it with you forever?

That heavy suitcase of past pain you're holding onto is doing nothing but dragging you down in your present.

Whoever hurt you has most likely moved on with their lives, so forgiveness is how you can finally allow yourself to move on with yours. The sooner you let go of your baggage, the sooner you'll create space to allow yourself to move towards a successful life on your terms.

Once I committed to practicing forgiveness, I carved out a morning to myself and started revisiting old memories. The idea was to reframe how I saw these memories by forgiving whoever or whatever was involved... and letting go.

I wrote down a list of all the experiences in my life that still stirred up feelings of pain. No experience was too big or too small. The important thing was to put it all down on paper. I wrote who was involved, how the experience played out, and why I felt hurt. I didn't go in chronological order as I wrote, I just put pen to paper and let my memories come through from elementary school all the way up through adulthood. Unsurprisingly, the first time I did this exercise, I ugly-cried as I scribbled a fair share of pages in my journal.

When I could no longer think of anything else, I went through each experience and decided what I needed to do to let it go. A handful required reaching out to others to have some hard, honest conversations years later. But most of them I went through one by one, held the memory in my head, and said to each one out loud...

I forgive you.

I'm sorry.

I love you.

Admittedly, this was weird the first time through. Even when I could feel the intention behind the words was half-hearted, I committed to saying the words over and over — almost like a chant. And when I'd gone through every memory I could think of, I went back through each one again. Only this time, I forgave myself for the part I had to play in each experience. I've done this exercise a few times since, and each time the list of pages in my journal gets smaller.

Warning: every ounce of you will want to skip this step. Don't. You can't move onto the next chapter of your life if you're held back by your past.

Our minds, bodies, and hearts carry the memories of a lifetime with us. It's why we can still recall the voice of our favorite grade school teacher or the smell of our grandma's perfume years later. So imagine the unresolved pain you've been carting around for years. It's been piling up and weighing you down. Stop running from it and confront it. Feel each bit of pain to heal it fully. Then let it all go — for good.

In the wake of all that pain, you'll finally have space to let yourself grow. Only then can you live the life of your dreams.

Love yourself for the person you are and for who you are on your way to becoming.

CHAPTER 6

ARE YOU LISTENING TO YOUR INNER VOICE?

"It is through science that we prove, but through intuition that we discover."

-Henri Poincare

When it comes to defining the life you want to lead, you're gonna have to tune out the noise around you and tap into what you truly want.

But how can you hope to define success on your terms if you don't even know how to define it for yourself? How do you know where to draw the line between what you think is expected of you and what you genuinely desire?

To do so, you must understand and trust your intuition. Some people refer to it as their gut instinct, inner voice, inner teacher, inner wisdom, spiritual guide… whatever you choose to call it, you have it inside you, too.

In quiet moments, you may have felt it. A familiar knot in your stomach. A feeling in your chest when something isn't right. How many times have you just known something about a person or a situation, only to have your suspicions confirmed after the fact? You may have brushed it off as coincidence and looked outside yourself for answers – to others, to facts, to reason, and to hard evidence. You learned not to trust your inner voice because you grounded your understanding of the world in what you saw rather than what you felt.

Intuition shows up in different ways for everyone. It could appear as a voice, a feeling, or just a sense of "knowing". It could be a hunch, a fleeting impression, or a tug in your gut. However it shows up for you, it's time for you to give it space to speak to you.

Start by asking yourself, when was the last time you stopped to think about your deepest desire? When was the last time you simply stopped to *be* in the moment during a difficult time and find stillness to gain clarity?

You may be rushing so fast from one thing to the next that the idea of taking time for yourself feels impossible. You may be so focused on what society, friends, or family expects from you that to listen to what you truly want seems silly.

I'm not asking you to toss aside outside opinions completely, but rather consider adding your own inner voice to the mix. I'm not asking you to give up your Netflix binge, your downtime with friends or however you unwind after a long day, but rather think about how you can cultivate a practice that allows you to just *be* with yourself.

I wasn't taught to practice solitude. Growing up in a heavily extroverted culture like the US means you're constantly surrounded by people, places, and things competing for your time and attention.

I never learned to sit down quietly. I was always rushing to the next thing, running to the next activity. I always had a plan to see through, an event to attend or a place to be. It wasn't until my late 20s that I grew to actually like spending time on my own. In fact, I didn't realize I was an introvert until quite late in life. With that critical understanding, I learned to embrace solitude without feeling pressure to make plans or feel guilty for just… being.

The same is probably true for you. When was the last time you sat down, deliberately, and did absolutely nothing? I don't mean plopping on the couch and pulling out your phone or flipping on the TV. I mean genuinely sitting in silence. If you practice meditation or lie in Shavasana at the end of a yoga class you may get this in tiny spurts. But what would happen if you practiced solitude regularly?

You need to give yourself a way to just be — to learn to be comfortable in solitude. It's critical to help you listen to your inner voice regularly to understand what a successful life means to you. It empowers you to create your own peace of mind. And when you consistently create this space for yourself, the answers you're looking for will reveal themselves to you.

I found my love of solitude in my search for a morning practice as an entrepreneur. Ever the personal development junkie, I'd read that all the people I admired attributed their success to a morning routine. Journaling, meditation, yoga, running, getting up early, drinking this specific type of coffee or tea before starting their day... the options seemed endless. But the one thing they all had in common was carving out the first few hours of their day to be alone.

I decided to try it out to find what worked best for me. I used myself as a lab rat to test-drive different routines and measured their effect on my performance over the course of the day. I tried morning walks listening to podcasts and yoga in the afternoons. I tried the morning pages from Julia Cameron's The Artist's Way and the 5-Minute Journal. I tried bulletproof coffee and matcha tea. I tried intermittent fasting and juicing, jogging and running, barre and HIIT videos on YouTube. I tried forcing myself out of bed at 6am (that one definitely didn't stick).

It took me a few months to find a routine, but I'll tell you what I landed on: meditation, journaling and some type of exercise. I realized that before I sat down to write a client brand story or hop on back-to-back Zoom calls, I needed to have at least the first hour of the day to feel grounded in myself. Before I dedicate myself to my commitments and my to-do list, I start my day having nourished my mind, body, and spirit. And it's an energy I carry with me that allows me to show up more fully as myself wherever I go.

There's an expression in yoga that I love: root to rise. And that's what my morning practice currently does for me. It helps me root down to rise up as I show up for others, as a business owner, a strategist, a coach, a wife, a sister, a friend, and a teacher. More importantly, it helps me regularly listen to my inner voice and allows me to make decisions more intuitively as my day, month, and year goes on.

Whenever I'm about to make a big decision in my life or business, I know I can trust my inner voice to guide me because I've made a point to nurture it regularly, to tune out external forces or opinions when I need to, and to cultivate space for it to speak to me in the silence.

And it's a practice you can cultivate for yourself, too.

Tuning into your inner voice will allow you to answer the biggest questions in life for yourself:

- "Is this something I want to be?"
- "Is this something I want to do?"
- "Is this something I want to have?"
- "Is this aligned with who I am and who I want to be?"
- "Is this going to take me towards what I want or away from it?"

The answers you need are already inside you. You just need to clear the noise regularly to hear what they are and use that inner wisdom to guide you as you move forward.

Listening to your inner voice is like training a new muscle, especially when it's been underused for so long. With practice, you'll learn to recognize when fear is trying to drown it out. Fear keeps you playing small and sends its partner in crime – doubt – to keep you where you are.

Your inner voice encourages you to move through the world in a way that feels *good* to you. You're listening to your inner voice when you feel empowered, authentic and at peace with yourself and others. You'll notice that good people and positive experiences are easily drawn to you. When you tune out fear and tap into your intuition, you'll no longer feel stuck, unfulfilled, angry, and resentful. By listening to your inner voice, you become the creator of your life rather than a bystander.

Sometimes the inner voice offers a choice that's scary, making you hesitate and question the accuracy. But more often than not, the most difficult choices are the ones that launch you outside of your comfort zone toward a life filled with purpose, fulfillment, and joy. That's the magic space where you learn and grow the most — and where you'll define success on your terms.

CHAPTER 7

LOVE YOURSELF AS YOU ARE (AND FOR WHO YOU'LL BECOME)

"The greatest thing you'll ever learn is just to love and be loved in return."

-Nat King Cole

I remember the first time I heard the phrase "authentic self-love" and stifling a laugh. By that point, I was knee-deep in the personal development world, wading through self-help books around how to "find my passion" or "follow my bliss". The phrase "go love yourself" felt like yet another thing to add to the list of cut-rate Confucius clichés on how to live a better life.

But gutter mind aside, what the heck did all these people mean by self-love? Was I supposed to take bubble baths every night with cucumbers on my eyelids listening to a Spotify spa playlist? Did it mean having my nails done more often or flying to Bali to find my own inner-enlightened Elizabeth Gilbert?

I soon learned that going on a solo retreat or pampering yourself with a nice pedicure may be part of loving yourself — but that's just scratching the surface.

As it turns out, self-love, like forgiveness, is a practice to be cultivated. It's not a final destination. It's not something to check off the list every day like another item on your to-do list. Self-love is the foundation upon which you build the life of your dreams.

The road to whatever success looks like for you will not be easy. You'll fall flat on your face more than once. Your journey will not be a straight line. It will be full of pivots, disappointments, and near-misses. No matter what comes your way, you'll have to show up fully to experience the good and the bad. And you'll have to love yourself hard through it all.

Think about it...if you don't love yourself as you are right now, pre-glitz, glamour, and future fabulousness, how can you possibly expect to love yourself when you get there?

As I recovered from depression, I had to take a long, hard look at myself. I realized that I'd spent the better part of my life neglecting my own needs, putting myself last, and giving away my power to others. I gave away responsibility for my own happiness and was constantly seeking it elsewhere. I rarely spoke my mind. I created patterns in relationships that left me disappointed in others and in myself.

This realization launched me into a relentless search for what self-love looked like for me, both internally and externally. After embracing the practice of forgiveness, the next step was to unlearn and unbecome all the things that held me back from self-love.

I was forced to dig deeper than I ever had before. I had to evaluate my relationship with myself and how it affected how I showed up in my relationships with others. To my surprise, I discovered places where I'd abandoned myself completely, parts where I'd surrendered my joy and sense of self-worth to the outside world. I'd learned to make myself small to please others, to be outspoken but not too outspoken, to be pretty but not too pretty, to be smart but not too smart. Everything I did was through the filter of needing someone else's approval for what I did and how I acted. Everything I achieved or accomplished was done because it was what was expected of me, not because I chose it out of a place of love for myself.

The reason I wasn't living life on my terms was because my inner self-love container was so small, I wouldn't have been able to receive happiness or success at all.

When I started my path of self-discovery, I began living a life that looked unconventional to outsiders but internally, felt like the truest version of me I'd ever been. I quickly learned which relationships in my life mattered and were worth holding onto. I also learned just how well I'd trained certain people to disregard my feelings. As I grew into who I was meant to be and started to stand up for myself more, people in my life started to push back. They tried to hold onto their idea of who I used to be and keep me in my place. Which meant that as much as I loved them, I had no choice but to remove them from my life. As terrifying as it was letting go, it helped me move forward and experience a deeper love for myself and for those who stood by me.

Learning to love yourself for who you truly are will be one of your greatest quests in life. From working with business owners across all over the world, I've come across those who are always striving to be someone or something they're not. It's my job to encourage them to own who they are instead of becoming a caricature of themselves or parroting someone else they admire. In the process of finding their story, they learn to love and leverage who they are, and you can do the same.

Cultivating self-love means you become someone you can live with and love exactly as you are, no matter what. To understand what success looks like on your terms, you need to understand who you are. By accepting who you are and loving yourself unconditionally, you start to surround yourself with others who acknowledge your value and your worth. You won't waiver in your identity or your sense of self as you move through life.

You need to love the person you are, the person you'll become, and who you are in between as you are rewriting your story.

CHAPTER 8

THE HARD AS F*CK ART OF NOT GIVING A F*CK

"Care about people's approval, and you will always be their prisoner."

-Lao Tzu

So you're starting down this path towards uncovering who you are, understanding what success is on your terms, and beginning the journey to make it happen. You're turning up the growth mindset. Buying all the books. Signing up to walk on coals. You're (in some cases, literally!) on fire.

But what happens when the people around you aren't on the same plane? The people who've seen you in diapers all the way through to your college binge-drinking buddies — they have a very clear idea in their heads of who they think you are. Sometimes, we get lucky and as we're in the process of upgrading ourselves, we encourage and inspire others by example to do the same.

Unfortunately, more often than not, people will feel threatened by this version of you that you're trying to become and find a way to reel you back into the very iteration of yourself that you're trying to leave behind. So how do you maintain the relationships you've relied on up until this point?

Honestly? You're gonna have to learn to give less f*cks and stop wasting your precious time giving a single crap what other people think about you — even if they think they know who you really are.

But here's the truth…

Giving no f*cks is not an art.

Giving no f*cks is not subtle.

(Yes, I'm poking fun at the title of what is, in fact, a very good book.)

The last time I checked, most well-meaning, decent human beings have a LOT of f*cks to give about what people think. Especially when it comes to trusted friends, family, and loved ones who they depend on.

Let's put it another way. When I was little, my mom used to take my sister and me to Seafood City, a Filipino supermarket chain that had stores near us in Southern California. While she'd stand at the counter ordering oxtail for Kare-Kare or catfish for Sinigang, my sister and I would wander over to the live seafood section. Somehow, I'd always end up in front of the plastic bucket with live crabs. I'd reach for the tongs to grab one of them, and all the other crabs in the bucket would surround it and hold it back with their pincers to keep their soon-to-be-boiled friend down in the bucket with them. (Sorry, vegans.)

My mom used to call this the "crab mentality". She taught us that sometimes, other people will react negatively when we decide to step out and do something different. Like the crabs in the bucket, when people see us aiming for something extraordinary that's outside of their comfort zones, they'll try to hold us back.

You're not in high school or college anymore. There is no popularity contest where you win a crown for being the fakest, conform-iest version of yourself to fit a mold you didn't even like being placed on you to start with.

We're talking about your LIFE, my friend.

The only crown you should be worrying about is the one you've created for yourself as monarch of your destiny.

:: mic drop ::

Seriously… think back to your teens and twenties. How many waking hours of your day did you spend stressing over what other people thought of you? What other people would think of your hair, your looks, your sneakers, your bookbag, the way you walked, the way you talked, the shows you watched, the books you read, the people you were seen with? Hoo-wee, I'm getting light-headed just thinking about it! We've all been there – evaluating where you were and how you acted on the social food chain was all about your survival.

As we age, if we're lucky, we start to loosen our grip on our obsession with what others think of us. But even if we do, it's tough for us to let go of it completely. So, we settle for an ordinary, acceptable version of life that doesn't rock the boat for those around us.

But if you wanted an ordinary life, you wouldn't be reading this book.

Since the dawn of time, nothing extraordinary was ever accomplished from the cushiness of someone's comfort zone. The truly successful outliers risked failure, ridicule, rage, ostracism, even death.

I'm not asking you to risk your life here. But I *am* asking you to risk the millions of opinions that'll be hurled your way as you start to rebuild yourself and create your dream life.

So how can you let go of caring so much about what others think of you?

1 - Control the things you can

You're responsible for what you say and do. You're *not* responsible for how others choose to respond to you as you level up your life.

What other people think about you, even if they claim to know and understand you, has more to do with them and their hang-ups that are being triggered by your decision to commit to a higher purpose for yourself.

Even with the best intentions, you will be misinterpreted, misunderstood, misread, misjudged. Criticism will be inevitable. If you know your heart is in the right place and that you're genuinely trying your best with what you have, then you know the harsh words thrown your way have no basis in your reality.

How you choose to respond to criticism is completely up to you.

2 - Seek your own approval

It's not just criticism you have to worry about. It's just as important not to get caught up in others' praise.

...say what?

Listen, there's nothing wrong with accepting a compliment. It's nice to hear someone cheering you on when it feels like everyone around you is constantly questioning your moves towards your dream life.

But there is a problem when you get into the habit of seeking outside approval for the steps you're taking. If you depend on others to validate your decisions, you're in danger of associating your self-worth with the external validation of others. So do not base your self-worth on what others think. No matter what others say to you, good or bad, own your decisions with confidence. If you're trying your best and you're connected to the *why* behind what you're doing, you can hold your head a little higher and take pride as you move through life.

3 - Create a circle of trust

Figure out who's in your corner as you begin this journey towards becoming who you were meant to be. Maybe you'll get lucky and it's someone who you've known your whole life who will love and support you unconditionally. But you may have to leave the herd you've known to find a new tribe of people who understand you and can reflect your new reality back to you.

Whether it's a spouse, partner, sister from another mister, or a biz bestie, make a list of the people who you know will hold you accountable. They're the circle of people whose opinions *do* matter; whose input you can trust will be given to you from a genuine desire to see you succeed in life. No matter what, they'll give you constructive criticism and constructive praise.

When you hit a wall and you struggle to remember why you started, when you doubt everything you're doing and you're a massive, teary ball on the floor crying a second Nile River into existence…these are the ride-or-dies that will hold it down for you.

They'll hold a mirror up to you to show you what you can't see in yourself. They'll give you the information you need at the time you need it most. They'll hug you when you're down, they'll celebrate you when you're up, and they'll call you out on your BS when you're losing your way.

You'll be connected to your truest self because they'll help you remember who that is.

4 - Love yourself

No matter what people say, think, or do to try and discourage you, have faith in who you are and the path you're taking.

Love yourself for the person you already are and for who you are on your way to becoming.

CHAPTER 9

THERE'S NO RIGHT WAY TO FIND YOUR PURPOSE

"Authenticity is a collection of choices that we have to make every day. It's about the choice to show up and be real. The choice to be honest. The choice to let out true selves be seen."

-Brené Brown

There's a reason most marketing and self-help books focus on words like "purpose" and "authenticity". It's something we all aspire to discover, be, do or have. We admire the people who own what makes them unique, who share who they are with the world without apologies, and who seem to have found their calling in life. They operate as their truest, highest selves because they are absolutely certain in who they are. #ZeroF*cksGiven

Understanding what your purpose is will be the difference between living a life of your dreams and wandering aimlessly. It's the difference between feeling happy, fulfilled, and achieving success on your terms... and feeling stuck inside a cage built by your own insecurities, fears, and tired excuses.

Every single one of us is here for a reason. We each have unique, valuable gifts to share with the world in the time we're given on this planet. And when we discover what we were meant to give, that's when the real magic begins. We start to live our lives on purpose *with* purpose.

So how do we find out what we're meant to do and who we're meant to be?

If you find yourself struggling to find clarity on what you want in life or feel like you're settling for less than you know you deserve, you have to start by uncovering answers that are already inside of you. Maybe you've already found your dream career but you're looking to take things to the next level. Maybe you're clueless and confused about where to start and how. No matter where you are, zooming out regularly and evaluating where your life is going is a valuable way to make sure you're always on the right path.

Keep in mind, there is no one right way to find your purpose. We're all at different places on our journey, but we're all heading for the same destination: a place where we feel most joyful, most alive, and most like ourselves.

And though I'm not gonna be able to hand you your life purpose on a platter, I'll share some of my favorite exercises from teachings I've picked up on my own journey. Hopefully one of them will trigger the right question to help you get clear on who you are and what your calling is:.

1 - Ask how you want to be remembered

Most of us don't like thinking about death. It freaks us out. But embracing the fact that our lives are finite and thinking about how we want to be remembered is a useful exercise to help us find our purpose. It helps us zero in on what's actually important in our lives.

I lost my Lola (grandmother in Tagalog) on July 3, 2017. At her funeral, no one was talking about how big her house was or whether she had a perfect attendance record at her job. Her legacy was defined by the people whose lives she touched, how her actions made people feel, and how much she loved her family.

When you imagine the end of your life, what will your legacy be? What stories will people tell about you when you're gone? What will your obituary say? How will you show up in your life today and every day to work towards making that legacy a reality?

2 - See yourself through the eyes of an admiring stranger

Imagine yourself as if you were someone just meeting you for the first time. What do they see in you? What strengths and talents do they admire in you? When do they see you enjoying yourself the most? What resources, opportunities, and connections do they see that are available to you?

If this stranger is only able to see the best in you, everything you do will seem new and exciting for them. They don't see your past or your baggage. They aren't limited by your worries or weighed down by your doubts.

Write down all the amazing things they're able to see in you.

All too often, we get caught up in our own limitations instead of embracing our limitless potential. Sometimes zooming out entirely helps us become more aware of how incredibly fortunate we are and opens our eyes to possibilities and potential we've been incapable of seeing.

3 - Create your purpose hypothesis and start before you're ready

A lot of us put pressure on ourselves to discover the one big thing we're here for. But the truth is, our purpose will evolve over time as we discover more about who we are. So if the whole "life purpose" idea is bumming you out, try answering a more manageable question right now:

"What can I do with my time that's important and meaningful to me?"

Think back to what you loved as a child and how you can reconnect with that. Think about moments in your life when you were doing something you were naturally good at and imagine how it would make you feel to make space for it more often. Think about who you could serve with your talents and how you can reach them.

Try filling out this sentence: "I help [group of people] achieve [desired outcome]."

Even if you don't create a business around your purpose, knowing who you want to help and the transformation you'd like to help them achieve is a valuable exercise. The happiest, most successful people in life found their purpose by finding what they were good at and using it to serve others. I suspect the same is true for you.

My purpose hypothesis used to be, "I help entrepreneurs find their story to grow their audiences." As my business grew, I came across founders that didn't fall into the typical "quit my cushy corporate job to start a business" narrative who also deserved to have their story heard. I knew that for every story shared from non-traditional business owners, our definition of what entrepreneurship can look like expands, creating a more inclusive world for us all. So my purpose hypothesis eventually evolved into, "I help underrepresented entrepreneurs achieve visibility to grow their audiences online."

Once you've written both of those things down... get out and test it. Instead of holding fast to this idea of your purpose like a defined mission statement, approach it like an experiment. Test it. See if it feels good or if it doesn't. Tweak it accordingly.

It's more fun this way than putting an insane amount of pressure on yourself to discover the reason behind your existence. Your purpose will reveal itself through taking action and then deciding the next right thing to do.

4 - Listen to your inner voice

As you learned in Chapter six, our intuition is one of our greatest assets. If you're looking for insights into who you are and what you're here on this planet to do, look no further than your inner voice. Our subconscious already holds the answers to the questions we're asking, we just have to tune out the noise to let those insights simmer to the surface.

Carve out five minutes a day to just be with yourself. No distractions. No excuses. Maybe it's first thing in the morning, on a five-minute walk around your building, or right before you go to bed. When you sit in silence, you allow the answers you already have inside you to reveal themselves.

5 - Stop waiting for a magic ah-ha!

For some reason, we all subscribe to this idea that our life's purpose will somehow be revealed to us out of thin air. That thunderbolts and lightning (very, very frightening!) will strike us, the heavens will part, and a choir of angels will sing in unison the one piece of soul-defining insight we've been waiting for.

Most of us end up paralyzed, waiting for this passion or so-called purpose to appear.

Let yourself off the hook if you haven't found the one big thing you're here to do. In fact, you probably don't have just *one thing* you want to do. Embrace that this is totally acceptable and normal for most of us.

But at a certain point, you're gonna have to stop meditating on what you're meant to do and get out and do it. You don't have to know exactly where you're going right away. You just need to follow what feels right to you now, then the next thing, then the next.

6 - Dive in at the deep end

Ask yourself what you fantasize about doing or being most. What would you do if you knew you couldn't fail or had an unlimited supply of money at your disposal? Is it performing your heart out from a Broadway stage? Is it opening up a homemade popsicle stand on the beach? Is it building schools around the world for kids who need access to education? Is it taking your children on a trip around the world, living in a different country every few months?

No matter how "out there" or ridiculous it may seem to you now, your wildest fantasies can help you uncover what you really want out of life. And chances are you're avoiding what you truly care about because of fear wrapped up in excuses.

Now that I've given you all these strategies to reflect on and find your purpose, it's time to switch gears entirely and dive in head first.

Yes, deciding to do something different will be hard. Yes, you'll suck when you start. You'll have no clue what you're doing right away. You'll have to make a few sacrifices and struggle a bit on the road to getting what you truly desire. You're gonna have to embarrass yourself in some shape or form, often repeatedly.

But what if you had the courage to leave those insecurities behind once and for all, and just went for it? What if you decided that today was the day you were going to live the life you always wanted, people's opinions and society's expectations be damned?

Now *that's* living on purpose.

7 - Love yourself

Honor where you are on this journey without judgment. As always, love yourself for the person you are and for who you are on your way to becoming.

CHAPTER 10

TUNE OUT TO TUNE BACK IN

"Have the courage to follow your heart and intuition. They somehow already know what you truly want to become. Everything else is secondary."

-Steve Jobs

It never ceases to amaze me how much time and energy we collectively waste every day.

We replay our dramas from past hurts. We chase one shiny object after another. We fuss over zits or unwanted facial hair. We chide ourselves for having too much fat on one part of our body or not having enough muscle on another. We seek out the praise of others. We dissect the lives of people we envy, trying to gain their approval or tear them down. We whine about the lack of good Wi-Fi, the weather, the traffic. We get stuck watching reruns of the past or stressing about the future and we forget the glorious present that's right in front of us.

You're plugged into noise to numb your pain. And it's not your fault you got this way.

When we're born, we trust our instincts. It's what helps us babble, crawl, and eventually teeter-totter into our first tentative steps. We know how to eat when we're hungry, to sleep when we're tired, to not care what others think when we fall down or sing off-key. We know how to play, laugh out loud, create, and be ourselves without holding back.

But over time, we start absorbing the messages we receive from our parents, our teachers, and society at large. We learn from, respond to, and are shaped by what we're told to do to survive in the world. We absorb fear, self-doubt, and the false, limiting beliefs that chip away at our true selves. We wind up hurt and start to carry that physical and emotional pain around with us. We start to numb our pain with booze, drugs, sex, food, TV... or whatever poison we've chosen.

Everyone has a past. Everyone has a story of failure. Everyone has a trial, tribulation or tragedy that knocked them down, leaving us questioning whether or not it's possible to move forward.

At a certain point, we all come to a crossroads. We can decide to settle for mediocrity or we can unlearn everything we've been taught as true, start over, and relearn everything we already knew when we came into the world.

Imagine what our world would be like if we spent less time blaming others, feeling threatened and fighting over petty differences... and spent more time accepting one another as the result of loving ourselves more?

Imagine how different *your* life would be if you woke up every morning absolutely certain of your worthiness, your enoughness, and your ability to leave your mark on this planet. If you told self-doubt and self-loathing to scram so you could be, have, and do whatever your heart wanted most.

You can't decide where you came from. But you can always decide where you go from here.

And it starts with you making a conscious decision to stop listening to the noise that you're using to fill in where you feel empty, to drown out where you feel inadequate, to cover up where you feel "less than" or small.

Here are a few ways you can begin tuning back into who you already are:

1 - Appreciate yourself

You are not here on this Earth by accident. Everything you've lived through, every mistake you've made, every win you've celebrated, every time you fell flat on your face... it's all made you who you are.

So, if you're going to blame your past for your current reality, blame it for the good things, too, because you wouldn't be strong if you hadn't faced hardship. You wouldn't know joy if you hadn't experienced loss or sadness. You wouldn't know love if you hadn't known heartbreak.

Thank your past and accept that all the times you let yourself down were lessons for you to learn from. And thank yourself for your desire to create the life you desire today.

2 - Speak to yourself more kindly

How would you talk to a friend who had lost a job, or misplaced their keys, or felt like they were a failure? Would you yell at them and tell them they were an embarrassment? Would you hold their mistake over their head until the end of time?

Or would you listen calmly, reassure them gently, and help them approach the lesson from a place of kindness and love?

Now talk to yourself like you would to a friend. Whenever perfectionism or self-criticism works its way up into your brain, gently tell it to move aside and welcome that friendly, kind voice to speak to you instead.

3 - Do more of what you love

One of the reasons I burned out early on is because I developed an unhealthy obsession with the results instead of the progress, with the destination instead of the journey. And I'm not alone. We're encouraged as a society to only pursue passions that we can monetize, to force a decisive conclusion instead of embracing the lesson, and to think that anything less than fame and fortune means we've failed.

Here's a radical idea…

Why don't we just do what we love for the pure joy of it? With absolutely no attachment to the outcome? (I know, mind-blowing, right?)

Maybe there's a project you've been putting off because you're scared it won't look like what you've seen on Pinterest. Just start.

Or maybe there's a painting class you've been saying you'll attend but you're scared of looking like a complete idiot. Just sign up.

To steal from an improv class I attended in college, turn your "No, but…" into a "Yes, and…"

The more you find yourself in situations that are wayyyy out of your comfort zone, the more you stretch yourself, the more you face your fears. Which means the more space you'll make for joy in your life without feeling pressure to perform or meet anyone's expectations but your own.

4 - Stop comparing yourself to others

Most of us spend more time than we should comparing ourselves to others. It starts in school and in sports. But as we got older, we began comparing other things: job titles, degrees, income level, house size, countries we've visited, and other worldly successes.

We can compare ourselves to each other on just about anything. But once we begin down that road, we never find an end. It's nothing but a one-way ticket to permanent unhappiness and it keeps us in a space of *lack* instead of a space of gratitude for what we already have.

We typically compare the worst we know of ourselves to the best we assume about others. Remind yourself that nobody is perfect. What people share publicly is usually just the highlight reel of their lives. Someone who looks like they "have it all figured out" is struggling with the same things we all do behind the scenes: insecurity, doubt, fear, sadness, loss, and every other emotion. I'm not telling you this to revel in their pain but rather to remind you that they're just as human as you are. Yes, even the most successful people you look up to because #NewLevelSameDevil.

Instead of focusing on what they have and what you don't, appreciate what's in front of you. Your gifts, talents, successes, experiences, and value are entirely unique to you and your purpose in this world. They can never be properly compared to anyone else. Every second you waste worrying that "you haven't gotten where you need to be yet" and looking at "how far ahead they are" is a second you could use to figure out what you want your life to look like.

And if you need to compare with anyone, compare with the past version of yourself. Commit to growing a little bit each day physically, emotionally, spiritually, and intellectually, and to celebrating each achievement, no matter how small.

5 - Forgive yourself

A mentor of mine once said, "Regrets are impossible as long as you make the best decision you can with what you have in front of you."

You today would probably go back to you yesterday and go, "What the heck do you think you're doing?!" before you started that doomed relationship with a narcissist, that horrible job with a slave-driver boss, or that pivotal life decision that took you to the opposite side of the world.

But since time travel is still science fiction and not science fact... forgive yourself. For every mistake you made, you gained more wisdom for your present and future.

6 - Learn to love your own company

When was the last time you consciously paused? When you didn't rush to reach for your phone or call up a friend or add more noise instead of just... sitting still?

Up until my early 20s, I was always rushing to *do* the next thing instead of just *be* with myself. I learned to let go of the pressure I put on myself to fill my social calendar to prove to 15-year-old me from high school that I wasn't a loser and a loner as an adult. I learned to crave meditation, yoga, solo walks with my thoughts and a podcast, journaling, or even spoiling myself with a bubble bath and a face mask. When I learned to take time to recharge instead of filling my days to the brim, I learned to love my own company. (Fist bump to my fellow INFJ's!)

Even if you thrive on being with people or you fall somewhere squarely in the middle of the introvert-extrovert spectrum, there's nothing wrong with a little solo downtime. In fact, there are lots of ways to find quiet in the busyness of life.

Turn off the phone. Shut off the TV. Take some time and space for yourself. I'll cover some specific self-care practices you can incorporate later in the book. But for now, challenge yourself to carve out a bit of time for yourself, even if it's just closing your eyes and sitting still for five minutes.

7 - Love yourself

You are worthy. You are enough. Love yourself for the person you are and for who you are on your way to becoming.

CHAPTER 11

ROOT DOWN TO RISE UP

"Solitude is where I place my chaos to rest and awaken my inner peace."

-Nikki Rowe

Self-care. Self-love.

They've become buzzwords and hashtags for a reason. With our increasingly noisy world, our inflated task list, and so many things competing for our attention, we often put "me time" on the bottom of our priorities. And when we are alone, the first thing we reach for is… you guessed it… more noise.

When I became a personal development junkie in my early twenties, I began to study the best practices of successful people. I knew that success left clues, so I got my hands on every article and autobiography I could find. I wanted to know how they were able to make the most of their hours to achieve successful lives on their terms. For some reason, I thought that they were all superheroes that had managed to optimize every single minute of their day for maximum productivity.

So what I discovered surprised me. They had the same 24 hours in the day that we all do, and how they each chose to spend it was entirely unique to them and their lifestyles. There wasn't a formula for being successful that I could just magically replicate in my own life to achieve the same results. It didn't matter if they were early risers or weren't, had families or didn't, started rich or didn't, were extroverted or introverted, worked from home or traveled often.

But there was one thing they all had in common...

Every single person I learned about cited regular alone time as the key to getting it all done. Some started the day journaling and meditating. Others ended their days with a good book before bed. Most of them credited exercise or some type of physical movement with keeping them sound in mind and body. Those who truly mastered their time made sure they fed their mental, physical, and spiritual needs before they started their day.

So, as I shared in Chapter six, I tried out different methods. They ranged from secular (freehand journaling) to woo-woo spiritual (crystals scattered around my home office). I would try everything out for a month or two, assess how I felt, evaluate, then slightly tweak my routine based on my conclusions. Later on in this book, I'll give you some examples of what I've tried so you can test different options for yourself and see what works for you.

Now I'm not asking you to become a monk or a hermit in the pursuit of a life of your dreams. But I *am* encouraging you to learn to love your own company.

Making regular time to breathe, to sit, and just be is a good thing. Even if you're a single parent juggling three jobs or an executive running a company, you can find the bare minimum of five minutes in your day to just sit with yourself. Not everything is an emergency that requires our immediate attention. And self-care isn't selfish — it's vital for your well-being.

More often than not, it takes a wake-up call like I had to notice the effect of putting self-care on the back burner. We have a big presentation to prepare at the office, a million things to do for our kids, or a freelance client deadline to meet. So we cancel that dance class. We say no to social engagements. We skip meals. We sacrifice on sleep. But eventually our mental, physical, and emotional health pay the price, often with serious consequences. I'm a big advocate for cultivating self-care because I know all too well what's at stake if you don't.

I founded my business to create a lifestyle that allowed me to keep my depression at bay and to help others create lives on their own terms by leveraging the power of their stories. Being an entrepreneur brings its own set of challenges, but whether the work day ends at 4pm or 10pm (to accommodate my US-based clients) I've baked "me time" into my schedule as a non-negotiable. For me, it isn't about creating a strict routine but rather creating space to tune into my inner voice regularly.

And that's ultimately what my wish is for you. Because without the solid foundation of knowing, accepting, and loving who you are, your house of cards will come crashing down on you pretty quickly. If you take nothing else away from this book except a deep desire to sit with, be, and love yourself more than you currently do, then you have what it takes to set yourself up for the life of your dreams.

But because I'm also about giving you concrete ways to turn inspiration into action, I'm gonna walk you through specific practices you can start cultivating today.

SECTION 2

RECLAIM

PRACTICE #1: JOURNALING

"The starting point of discovering who you are, your gifts, your talents, your dreams, is being comfortable with yourself. Spend time alone. Write in a journal."

-Robin Sharma

Journaling is a great practice for your own self-reflection and tuning into what you really want out of life. Successful people all over the world reflect daily and learn from their life experiences by keeping a journal including J.K. Rowling, Eminem, and Oprah. I knew that it was a valuable practice, but I never knew how to incorporate it into my life, thinking I was "too busy" to do it. Until I read one, incredible book – The Artist's Way by Julia Cameron. It's a book that teaches world-wary artists to get back onto the path of creativity, away from the fear that holds them back.

I wasn't what you'd consider a traditional artist, but I gave it a shot anyway. As I dove into the book, I learned that any act of creation or honing of a skill is art, even if it doesn't fit into what we typically think of when we hear the word "artist". Cameron argues that even if you're not a painter, a sculptor or gifted at playing an instrument, you can cultivate a practice of creativity.

One of the cornerstones of The Artist's Way is the Morning Pages. The actual exercise is pretty simple: find a notebook or journal of some kind, grab a pen or pencil, something that's comfortable for you to write with, get up a little bit earlier every morning, and write for three whole pages. Sounds easy, right?

But like with everything, the newness of the exercise wears off and there comes a day that you don't feel like writing. The challenge then is to write anyway. You might start writing and feel like you can't fill three pages, it's too hard. But fill all three anyway. The magic comes from pushing yourself to fill all three. It doesn't even matter what you write either. You could write down what dreams you had the night before, what you're currently worried about, the sounds of your cat scratching around in the litter box, the chores you don't want to do, the way your coffee tastes, a grocery list, a to-do list, affirmations... the choice is yours.

My favorite part of the Morning Pages is that by the very practice of repetition, I learned to enjoy spending time with myself. I learned to censor myself less and found clarity and confidence in bringing my own voice to the surface. I didn't care what I wrote because I knew no one else was reading it. I learned to let the words spill out and let go of judgment, writing exactly what was on my mind without worrying whether or it was too petty, silly or crazy-sounding. And I found that my capacity for uncensored, confident self-expression spilled over into my day-to-day life.

The best part? Morning Pages will keep you honest in a way that nothing and no one else will. If there's something you've been less than happy with about your life or career, they'll reflect those unfulfilled hopes and dreams back to you. And eventually you'll start to see those ideas pop up so often in your practice, you'll have no choice but to do something about it.

It's no exaggeration when I say it helped heal me and embrace a more creative, playful side of myself. And it's a practice I plan on returning to whenever I need inspiration or I'm struggling to see what my next steps are.

Eventually, I stopped writing the full three pages and started writing once a day in my journal even if it was just one page. If I forgot to write in the morning, I'd write in the afternoon or evening before bed. For the days I was in transit and forgot to bring my journal with me, I used the Day One Journal app on my phone to scribble down random thoughts or get something off my chest to gain perspective. It didn't matter to me that I wasn't "following the instructions" — I just cared about writing and enjoying the process.

Recording your thoughts in a medium outside your own head clears out that cache and makes way for new ideas and ways of thinking. Your mind becomes quieter, it stops returning to the same worn-out mental loops over and over, and you can begin to think more clearly.

Journaling also helps you gain a valuable perspective on your past and do what psychologists call "reframing your personal narrative". When you revisit and reflect upon your thoughts and experiences you are, in effect, telling your own story. Journaling helps us clarify and find new meaning in these narratives.

If you want to start journaling (Morning Pages or otherwise), here are a few tips to help you:

1 - Keep a journal beside your bed

Whenever I decide I want to incorporate a new habit, I try to make it as easy as possible to start. In this case, it was putting a journal beside my bed so I'd do it first thing in the morning. Whenever my alarm goes off, I can prop myself up on a pillow against my headboard and start writing before my feet hit the floor.

If you journal first thing in the morning, you know it will get done. Plus, when you're waking up, you're able to tap into your creativity and your intuition more. Writing when your brain is fresh will also help you channel insights and ideas onto paper without the noise of your to-do list and other outside inputs. Studies have even shown that writing things out by hand improves memory and encourages deeper thinking and reflection.

2 - Don't censor yourself

This journal is for your eyes only. Don't put pressure on yourself to come up with prolific prose or poetry. Use correct sentences or don't. Use punctuation or don't. If you misspell something or your grammar is off, don't go back and correct it. Just write.

The point of journaling is to learn to let go of your need to find an outcome. You're not writing for someone else's consumption, so say whatever you want without judging. Get your thoughts on paper. Don't edit; just write.

3 - Write, draw, or rant about whatever you'd like

You also don't have to write about your thoughts and feelings. If you're more artistically inclined than I am, you can fill your journal with doodles and daydreams.

Remember, this journal is your tool of self-expression – fill it up however you'd like. The point is to take a moment to write or draw and enjoy the action of doing so.

4 - Find a structure that works for you

Some of us look at a blank page and freeze up. Maybe you need a bit more structure in how you approach journaling. Try following daily writing prompts like the ones outlined in The Artist's Way. Or answer the same five questions every day.

There's no one "right" way to do it — there's only the way that feels right for *you*. Giving yourself some structure in what you write makes it easier to stick with the habit instead of getting overwhelmed with the possibilities. Experiment and find out which approach works best for you.

5 - Use a journaling app

In an ideal world, we would wake up first thing in the morning to absolute peace and quiet, curl up with our journal and a steaming cup of tea, and scribble away in our journal to our heart's content. But the demands of the day are real, and not all of us have the luxury of time.

The last thing I want is for you to think of journaling as another thing to stress you out. So let's make it easy for you. If you really can't imagine journaling with a pen and paper every day, try using a journaling app. If I have a particularly crazy month where I'm on the go, I can pop open the Day One app on my phone while on the Madrid metro or from my seat before take-off. You can do the same on your lunch break, commuting to work on the train or while waiting for your friend to arrive for drinks.

6 - Take time to pause

If you're anything like I was, writing a journal can feel like a waste of time. Try and resist the desire to rush through it to get to the next thing, especially when life is at its busiest. The practice of journaling can actually save you both time and stress by clearing your mind and clarifying your thoughts. Treat it as an investment in your productivity rather than something that detracts from it.

7 - Love yourself

As you journal, you may find that some things bubble up to the surface that you didn't expect such as past pains, traumas, and hurt. This is normal. If this happens, don't suppress them or run away. Use it as an opportunity to explore your feelings and reframe them if necessary. In my experience, breakdowns always happen before breakthroughs. Love yourself through the process.

So whether it's Morning Pages, downloading an app, or grabbing a fresh new notebook, start journaling regularly. Commit to writing something down every day for 30 days without censoring yourself and with an open mind. If you can get through a month of writing, I know you won't want to stop. You'll find yourself thinking clearer, being more creative, and confidently using your own voice. Eventually, you'll discover answers to what you want your life to look like by tapping into dreams you've kept hidden inside you.

And as always, love yourself for the person you are and for who you are on your way to becoming.

PRACTICE #2: MEDITATION

"Meditation is not a way of making your mind quiet. It's a way of entering into the quiet that's already there."

-Deepak Chopra

On paper, meditation sounds like the simplest thing we can do – sit still for a few minutes and try not to think about anything. And by doing so, you learn to gently push aside the thoughts that crowd your mind and tap into the inner voice that guides you in figuring out what you're meant to do next in life.

Another easy practice, right?

But then you sit down on the floor in a cross-legged position trying to channel Dalai Lama levels of zen and close your eyes… and not even 30 seconds into it, you're squirming and begging for the time to end.

Turns out that while at face value meditation sounds like the easiest thing in the world, it's *surprisingly* hard. Which is why you often hear it being referred to as a meditation practice.

In the same way you train your body through physical activity, meditation is how you train your mind. It's breathing. It's sitting still. It's learning to relax into the moment. And it's carrying that same presence, awareness, and mindfulness into the rest of your life.

I'm gonna be honest with you, when I first tried to give meditation a go, sitting with my eyes closed for five minutes felt excruciatingly long. My lower back and my hips were tight so sitting cross-legged was a challenge. Every time a thought came creeping into my head, I tried to swat it away like a fly and got angry at myself for not being able to "empty my mind". I found myself getting distracted by ambient noise like the construction on my street. By the time my phone alarm went off, I felt more frustrated than relaxed. And I didn't try meditation again for another year or so.

When I finally revisited meditation, I was looking to manage my stress. I was working two jobs in two languages in a foreign country and I found myself feeling anxious and struggling to sleep. I panicked because I had suffered from anxiety in high school without knowing what it was and didn't want to experience it again.

I went to see a doctor to try and find a way to manage it. He prescribed me medication to take when I felt myself getting trembly at work and it was small enough that I could pop one in discretely at my desk without anyone knowing. While it felt weirdly comforting to have those pills in my purse, I only ever took them once.

Let me be clear. I'm not a medical professional and I know that the well-meaning doctor was just giving me what I'd asked for – a way to help manage my anxiety. But since by that point I was familiar with the warning signs of burnout, I craved being able to support my mental health with more natural, sustainable practices instead of trying to numb the pain away at the first opportunity.

So, I decided to try meditating again. This time, I looked for guided meditations from different people on YouTube until I found ones I liked. Eventually, a friend recommended the Headspace app to me and I used their free 10-day course to help cultivate a practice. Knowing I had a soft voice to guide me, to help me breathe deeply, to welcome thoughts that entered my mind with grace and gently push them away as I continued to sit still, was enough to give me the foundation I needed to incorporate meditation into my daily routine.

If you're starting to get the urge to try it out, know this: there is no "right" way to meditate. Every person is different and every day is different. What I can say is that the practice of meditation has trained me to listen to my intuition and trust that my body will decide what feels good in that moment. Some days I meditate for 20 minutes, some days I meditate for five. Some days I meditate in the morning, some days I meditate in the evening. Some days I put on a guided meditation recording on Spotify, some days I sit still and breathe with my eyes closed until I feel like I'm ready to continue my day. There are still some days I forget to meditate entirely, but I still try to stay relaxed and breathe through tension instead of beating myself up about it.

And in case you're rolling your eyes at the fact that yet another book is telling you to meditate, hear me out.

Studies have shown that a regular meditation practice reduces stress, increases your concentration, and improves your circulation. On a personal level, I can credit meditation with helping me cultivate a quieter mind, a more open heart, and a stronger connection to my inner voice. That calm sense of clarity spills over into my work, my relationships, and everything else, and it's a sensation that keeps me grounded no matter how busy or hectic life gets.

I'm a recovering perfectionist, as Type A as they come, and I've been prescribed medicine for anxiety and depression at different times throughout my life. If I can see the benefits of meditation, you most certainly can, too.

There are plenty of resources out there on how to get started with meditating, but here are a few pointers:

1 - Start slow

If you're just starting your meditation journey, ease into it. Start with five minutes each day and set your phone timer to go off. Gradually increase the time as the weeks go by. If you find your monkey brain is making it hard for you to concentrate and you want a little more guidance, I can't recommend the Headspace app enough.

2 - Find your comfortable position

Look for a place where you won't be disturbed and allow yourself to settle into a position that feels good to you. You can meditate sitting or lying down (as long as you don't fall asleep!).

If you're sitting, find a comfortable spot where you can stay still for a few minutes. You can sit on the floor (using a pillow or cushion for support if your hips are tight) or sit upright in a chair with your feet resting on the floor. Try to maintain a straight spine without letting your body go too rigid.

You can meditate anywhere, but it's helpful to establish a corner of your home that you can revisit as you create a ritual for yourself.

3 - Close your eyes and focus on your breathing

Once you've settled into your meditation position, close your eyes and listen to the sound of your breath. You don't need to force it, just quietly observe as you breathe in and out. Don't worry whether it's slow, shallow, deep or consistent. Over time, as your mind calms down, your breath will, too.

As you focus on your breathing, your mind will probably start wandering. This is perfectly normal and you should be glad you've become aware of it. Rather than getting frustrated when you notice your mind has wandered, acknowledge the thoughts, let them pass, and gently bring your attention back to your breath. Repeat as often as necessary until your timer runs out.

When I first started meditating, I used to fidget a lot. My mind felt like a superhighway of speeding thoughts going 150mph. I would catch myself peeking at the timer counting down at the three-minute mark, then two minutes and 50 seconds — five minutes felt like an eternity! By week nine, I learned to move away from how I thought meditation should look ("sit still" and "keep my mind blank") to how it felt (gently acknowledging thoughts as they arise instead of forcing them to disappear). Now over two years into daily practice, I can sit for up to 20 minutes, twice a day without breaking a sweat.

4 - Let go of expectations

If you're sitting there, 30 seconds in wondering, "Am I doing this right?" because you haven't found some magical moment of enlightenment, don't worry.

Meditation is about cultivating awareness without judgment. Don't worry about setting expectations for what you'll "get out of it" when you sit down to meditate. You may experience profound insight during a session, you might be really bored. You might feel restless and impatient, you might feel calm and relaxed.

Your meditation practice is about embracing whatever is in the present moment. The benefits of meditation — greater self-awareness and self-control, increased calm and empathy — will emerge over time. But each day, each session, and each moment will be completely different. Trust in the process and learn to accept what is.

5 - Practice makes present

Regular practice is key for you to start seeing the benefits of meditation. Taking five minutes of your day to meditate can work wonders in the long run. After a while, your day will feel incomplete without it.

Choose the time of day that works best for you and your schedule. I tend to practice first thing in the morning after a walk or an at-home yoga session, but sometimes I meditate before I fall asleep. When I have to catch an early flight, I will meditate in transit on the way to the airport or when I've settled and taken my seat on the plane.

Work with what you have, find time for a mindful moment in your schedule, and make space for your meditation to happen. If you need an app to get started, I highly recommend Headspace or Insight Timer.

Ultimately, meditation will help you actively train your mind to dwell in the here and now rather than rehash past memories or fret about the future. Few of us tend to truly live in the present moment until we begin meditating. But once you start, it's like you've found the key that unlocks qualities and insights within yourself that have always been there for you to discover.

By regularly learning to be present and tapping into that inner voice, you'll discover the answers you need to create the life you've always wanted.

6 - Find joy in meditation

We've been taught to value doing > being. So something like meditation — which requires us to just be — can feel overwhelming at first. You think of a million other things you could be doing instead of sitting still. You get distracted and feel like you're "failing" and walk away. You find excuses to skip it altogether.

I stopped and started meditation about seven times before finally making it "stick". It was only when I started to truly enjoy meditating that I learned I couldn't live without it. It went from something on my "to-do list" to an oasis that was always available to me, that I could come back to whenever I needed to disconnect. I would open my eyes after each session filled with gratitude for the time I'd taken to recharge and move forward feeling lighter.

It's *your* meditation practice. Meditating doesn't have to look or feel a certain way, it just has to feel good to you. This time for yourself is not counterproductive. It's necessary for your health, well-being, and future happiness. Be grateful that you get to choose to spend this time enjoying your own company.

7 - Love yourself

Learn to love sitting still. Learn to love the moment-to-moment awareness. Learn to love your own company and the answers inside you will bubble their way to the surface.

Love yourself for the person you are and for who you are on your way to becoming.

PRACTICE #3: GRATITUDE

"Being grateful all the time isn't easy. But it's when you least feel thankful that you are most in need of what gratitude can give you: perspective. Gratitude can transform any situation. It alters your vibration, moving you from negative energy to positive. It's the quickest, easiest most powerful way to effect change in your life — this I know for sure."

-Oprah Winfrey

Thanksgiving is my favorite holiday. How could it not be? It's the perfect day to focus on the 4 F's of being Filipino: faith, family, friends, and food.

Every Thanksgiving, my family and I would travel up from Los Angeles to the San Francisco area where my grandparents, uncles, aunts, and cousins lived. Most of us were first- or second-generation immigrants, so the more "traditional" American dishes were supplemented with lumpia or eggrolls, pancit Canton or noodles, Filipino lechón or suckling pig, and, of course, piles of rice. (Growing up, I preferred the much juicier lechón to the turkey!)

But as a traditional Catholic family, we didn't just dive straight into the food when it was pulled out of the oven. We took a moment to gather around it and say a prayer before filling up our plates. We would stand, bow our heads, and listen as one of us would lead the blessing. It was always a moment to reflect on the year thus far, to give thanks for one another, to appreciate the amazing food we were about to have, and to express appreciation for our blessings.

That is what I think of when I think of gratitude.

So imagine my surprise when, in my quest to understand what a fulfilling life on your own terms looks like, the word "gratitude" kept coming up. More importantly, it was this idea of a "practice of gratitude" that left me a bit stumped.

But ever the researcher, I took a deep breath, tried to suspend my judgment and attempted to discover why gratitude was so important and why everyone in the personal development space was raving about it outside of Thanksgiving.

As it turns out, gratitude has more healing powers than I ever imagined possible. It's not as simple as just saying "thank you" whenever someone does something nice for you. While the idea of "gratitude" may sound cliché today, it's more straightforward than you might think.

Gratitude boils down to you having a true, genuine sense of appreciation for what you have in your life. For things big and small. For a blue sky above and for the air you breathe. For where you live, for the unquestioning devotion of your pet, for the gift of people who love you unconditionally.

It's easy in today's world to equate success with an endless chase for "more". We can easily take things for granted while we pursue the things we think we want. But gratitude is perhaps the most important key to finding both success and happiness. It's a filter to help us appreciate our past, celebrate the present moment, and dream about the future without getting bogged down in cynicism. Knowing what we appreciate in life means knowing who we are, what matters to us and what makes our days feel worthwhile. We cultivate a consistent positive state of mind and we feel more connected to the world around us and to ourselves.

Research demonstrates that focusing on what we are grateful for is a universally rewarding way to feel happier and more fulfilled. In one study, keeping a daily gratitude journal led to a 15% increase in optimism. Which makes sense, right? If we're grateful more often, we're more likely to feel more optimistic about our lives. We're more likely to feel more optimistic about our possibilities and our plans for the future. Optimism, in turn, makes us happier, improves our health, and has been shown to increase lifespan by as much as several years.

The benefits of gratitude extend far beyond what I initially imagined. Scientific studies have found that gratitude is associated with:

- Greater happiness
- More optimism and positive emotions
- New and lasting relationships
- Better health
- More progress toward personal goals
- Fewer aches and pains
- More alertness and determination
- Increased generosity and empathy
- Better sleep
- Improved self-esteem

I don't know about you, but those things all sound pretty appealing to me.

Gratitude is one of the easiest practices you can incorporate as quickly as right this second. So here are a few ways I incorporate it into my day to day to inspire you:

1 - Challenge your first response

When you start to tap into your inner voice, you may find she is more cynical than gentle. That's absolutely normal. You've been feeding yourself negative thoughts for so long that it's gonna take time to reprogram (which we'll cover in the next chapter). Arianna Huffington calls it the "obnoxious roommate" that's constantly criticizing you and looking for what's lacking.

Rather than letting it get to you by telling yourself what you supposedly can't do, be or have…try challenging that first response in your head: "Are things so bad? Am I capable of handling what's in front of me? Am I worthy of success?"

Then look for proof in your own experience that challenges what the obnoxious roommate is trying to tell you is "true". Actively think about how you turned things around. How you overcame a challenge. How you worked hard and were rewarded for your efforts.

This will help you be more thankful for what's in front of you and appreciate that you'll come out the other side of the situation with a lesson or a win.

2 - Be more accepting

Make a conscious effort to accept the things that are out of your control. The only constant in life is change, so the sooner you get used to it, the better you'll feel overall. Accept that you won't always get a say in the outcome of how things go and acknowledge that the only thing you can control is your reaction to it.

If you find yourself irritated by people around you, whether strangers or family members, embrace the idea that everyone is genuinely trying their best with what they have.

Please note: this does not require you to be some hippy-dippy, Zen'd out doormat, or to take abuse from someone willingly. But rather than trying to change others around you, focus on you. By accepting others, you learn to be more accepting of yourself.

3 - Practice mindfulness

Mindfulness is nothing more than the state of being conscious or aware of something, grounding yourself in the present moment, acknowledging and accepting things around you as they are. This can apply to your thoughts, your feelings or simply observing how your body feels from moment to moment. When we practice mindfulness, we allow our thoughts and feelings to move through us without taking over. And we become more appreciative of ourselves and our surroundings.

Sit down daily and think through five to ten things you are grateful for. Picture them in your mind and sit with that feeling of gratitude in your body. Doing this every day, even for just two minutes, will rewire your brain to be more grateful more often.

4 - Keep a gratitude journal

If visualization isn't your thing, you can bust out your journal and write those positive thoughts on paper. Writing down all the things you're thankful for can help you keep track of and refer back to the positives in your life.

While you are putting the pen to paper, you'll consciously think about the words you are writing instead of falling back into old feedback loops of negative, ungrateful thoughts. Plus, it's nice to look back on the month or year and be reminded of all of the things you have to be grateful for.

5 - Express your appreciation to others

Sometimes it's not enough to simply keep your gratitude to yourself. You can express that same gratitude you're cultivating in yourself to the people you care about. Let your partner know you appreciate them before you rush off to work. Thank your kids for remembering to take out the trash. Write a letter to an old teacher who made an impact on your life.

Expressing your gratitude for someone won't just make their day a little brighter — it can do wonders for upping your own levels of gratitude and happiness in the long run.

6 - Love yourself

Because you can't cultivate gratitude without appreciating yourself in the process. So love yourself for the person you are and for who you are on your way to becoming.

PRACTICE #4: AFFIRMATIONS

"Affirmations are statements going beyond the reality of the present into the creation of the future through the words you use in the now."

-Louise L. Hay

I can't do horror movies. There is literally no amount of money you can pay me to watch zombies, chainsaws, creepy clowns, blood, gore, and the like. In high school, I tried to "toughen up" and watch scary movies with friends. They thought it would be funny to watch how much I freaked out. But the experience of watching me cringe, curl up into a ball on my seat, and scream was scarier for them than the movie itself. So to my relief, we decided not to include me in any future horror movie outings. And I haven't seen one since.

The thing is, I'm an HSP (highly sensitive person) who also happens to be very visual. I can always rationalize in my head that the movie isn't really happening but the adrenaline of heightened visuals coupled with suspenseful music, the anticipation that a killer is around the corner, and seeing someone suffer and feeling their pain in my body is all too much for me.

If that wasn't bad enough, the images of the movie replay in my head for days and nights afterward. Every time my eyes close, my brain goes right to the scariest part of the movie I've just seen. I'm pulled right back to the fear I felt seeing it in the theater. So why would I pay money to watch something that doesn't just make me suffer for 90 minutes but for an entire week? No, thank you.

You don't have to be an HSP or a highly visual person to know that images stay with you. Songs stay with you. Bad news you hear on the radio stays with you. The inputs you receive on a daily basis are absorbed by your brain. They get fed into your conscious mind and eventually work their way into your subconscious.

Now imagine that you're forced to relive the worst movie you can imagine in your head, every day, for the rest of your life. How would that affect you? How would that change your ability to interact with others? How would that shape your perception of the world?

The fact is that many of us are replaying a bad movie version of our lives on loop. We re-watch our mistakes, our failures, and all the times we fell short. In the background, we play a bad soundtrack that tells us everything we've done wrong and what's wrong with us. It affects our confidence, it affects how we react to people and things around us, and it affects our ability to show up fully as ourselves.

Now imagine that instead, you ejected that bad VHS out of the VCR (yes, showing my age here) and popped in another movie instead. One that celebrates your accomplishments. One that highlights your strengths, your wins, and shows all your dreams being realized. One that shows how you're surrounded by people who love you and all the things you have to be grateful for in your life.

That's how affirmations work.

In the simplest terms, affirmations are positive sentences that you repeat to yourself to replace your limiting beliefs and reprogram your subconscious mind. They're so much more than the feel-good quotes you see on Instagram. They're words and phrases you say out loud to yourself or listen to on repeat to retrain your brain.

When you think a thought, your brain processes the information literally and prepares you for the action that should immediately follow your thought. It doesn't communicate in future or past-tense — it only understands what's happening in the present moment. Because your brain is constantly looking for clues to filter your environment and guide your actions, it will pick up on any available input and process it for you.

So, if given a choice: would you rather the information that entered your head was consistently positive or relentlessly negative?

And if affirmations still sound like unrealistic "wishful thinking" to you, try this perspective on for size...

Many of us do exercises to improve our physical health; affirmations are like exercises for a healthy self-esteem and outlook on life. What's more, affirmations help us challenge any deep-seated childhood fears, doubts from misguided teachers, or insecurities passed down from well-meaning parents that may be holding us back from creating successful, happy lives on our terms. With positive mental repetition, we can reprogram our thinking patterns so that, over time, we begin to think – and act – differently.

Affirmations can be a powerful tool to help you change your mood, state of mind, and manifest the change you desire in your life. But they work best if you can first identify the core belief that's getting in the way, then create an affirmation that helps you slowly replace that belief with one that empowers you.

To make affirmations that work for you, try the following techniques:

1 - Make a list of all the negative qualities you beat yourself up for

You can't change what you don't know needs fixing. So start by listing out the things you always tell yourself are your "worst" qualities. From things like your bad temper and how judgmental you are to any criticisms others have made that you've been holding onto – put it all down on paper. (This is where journaling will come in handy.)

Remember, no one is perfect, we all have flaws. Don't judge yourself or your siblings, parents, bosses or friends who may have unwittingly set off years of insecurities in you. Don't judge yourself for the emotions that will inevitably come up as you do a bit of digging. Simply make a note of them and look for a common theme, such as "I'm unworthy." This will be a great place to start creating affirmations that can help you reprogram your unconscious mind.

2 - Write the opposite of each negative as a positive

Even if you don't think it's true (yet), write down the opposite of what you think in a positive way. If you wrote "I'm unworthy" try "I'm loved and cherished". If you wrote "I hate my body" try "I love everything about my body". If you wrote "I'm hard on people" try "I see others as good people who are trying their best".

Make them specific and meaningful to you so every time you say them they'll resonate deeply within the core of your being.

3 - Make sure your affirmations only contain positive words

If your affirmation contains "don't," "can't" or "won't," reframe the affirmation to affirm what you're trying to achieve.

For example, instead of saying, "I won't increase my debt," a more positive choice would be, "I'm wealthy and prosperous."

4 - Make sure your affirmations are in the present tense

When you write your affirmations, write them in the present tense as though you are experiencing what you desire right now. For example, "I am happy" instead of "I will be happy". Your brain is eager to set you up for success, all you have to do is instruct it with the language that you speak.

5 - Make your affirmations relevant

Prepping for a job interview? Looking to find your dream partner or cultivate positive relationships? Want to run that marathon or get started exercising? Or earn more money than you do now? Craft your affirmation around what you want to focus on first and stick to it for at least two to three weeks.

6 - Repeat your affirmations as often as you'd like

There's no formula for how often or how many times you should repeat a positive affirmation. If there's something I really want to change, I'll repeat an affirmation to myself for five minutes straight first thing in the morning, during my lunch break, and right before bed.

I've heard of people repeating their affirmations 20 times, three times a day, or just once a day before they get out of bed. You can do it while you're shaving or putting on your makeup, making your coffee, or driving to your next errand. As long as you're focused when you repeat it, and you repeat it frequently, it will be successful.

7 - Love yourself as you progress

It will feel awkward at first, if not every day. It will feel untrue and you may feel like a cheesy fraud. But change starts from the inside and your belief in creating your dream life can only happen from a place of self-love.

So love yourself for the person you are and for who you are on your way to becoming.

Here are a few affirmations to guide you in creating your own:

- "I am successful, strong and satisfied."
- "I am a good person and worthy of love."
- "I deserve a wonderful life."
- "I effectively reach my goals."
- "I can handle anything that comes my way."
- "My life keeps getting better and better."
- "I am grateful for the love and light in my life."
- "I am just as important as anyone else."
- "I easily bring money and wealth into my life."
- "I feel wealth and abundance flowing toward me now."

Even if it feels untrue right now, the discomfort will motivate you to change and actively look for opportunities to transform your thoughts into reality.

PRACTICE #5: VISION BOARD

"What you focus on expands."

-T. Harv Eker

Something you should know about me: I feel immediate resistance to following anything that becomes mainstream. (Does that make me a hipster? Crap! That means I'm now mainstream. Oh, the irony… but I digress.) One of the things I avoided like the plague was The Secret and the Law of Attraction. The idea of manifesting sounded way too woo-woo for me.

I thought, you expect me to believe that sitting and envisioning myself on a pile of money on a luxury yacht means I wake up the next day with a yacht in my backyard? Pfffft, what a load of BS.

…until I manifested two things in rapid succession without even trying.

The first was in early 2018 when my husband had just started a job for a company with headquarters in Paris — the first city where I'd lived abroad before Madrid. I remember idly chopping onions for dinner one day and thinking, for a split second, how cool it would be if I could take Javi to Paris in the springtime… and show him the first place that sparked my wanderlust as a teenager.

Not even a week later, Javi called me on his lunch break practically bouncing on the other end of the phone. "Honey, you'll never guess what just happened at work today. Are you ready? They're sending me to…"

"...Paris!" we screamed into the phone at each other.

"I know this is gonna sound crazy," I continued, "but I don't feel surprised, I feel... almost as if I were expecting it to happen. Like... I thought about us going to Paris in the springtime last week while making dinner. And it's as if just thinking it for a nanosecond made it come true. I think this is what you'd call... half-assed manifesting?"

"...well whatever you did, it worked! When are we booking our flights?"

The second was in June 2018, only a few months later. I'd been having a solo pity party about how the Bruno Mars concert in Madrid had sold out within 48 hours of ticket sales going live a year earlier. He's one of the few artists on my bucket list that I want to see live in concert.

As Javi jetted out the door for work the morning of the concert, he said to me, "Well, who knows? Maybe you'll manifest another miracle."

Sure enough, t-minus four hours before the venue opened, I got a phone call. My friend on the other line asked, "Kay, how would you like to watch the Bruno Mars concert from the VIP section? My company gave me an extra ticket and my wife and I would love to have you join us!"

Another #HalfAssedManifesting for the win. Though this one I'll say was a joint effort between Javi and me.

I know, I know. The last-minute trip to Paris and the Bruno Mars concert may sound superficial and silly. But what struck me was that neither of these events had been on my radar, at least consciously, in the months and weeks leading up to when they happened. By that point, I couldn't deny that what I had focused on had, indeed, expanded. There was no logical or rational explanation for how either of those things could have happened. It was as if I had an internal antenna that took my literal thoughts, emitted a magnetized frequency, and drew in the exact thing those passing thoughts had asked for.

So I went from toe-dipping to waist-deep in the waters of "woo" to learn more about the Law of Attraction. (The rebel in me still backed up every New Age-y spiritual concept I came across with stats, studies, and science, of course.) I figured if I'm able to manifest thoughts into reality without heavily focusing on an outcome, what happens if I channel that energy into something I do want?

The LoA concept that came up repeatedly to "manifest with intention" was the vision board.

A vision board is a collage of visual images or words that represent the life you want to live. Quite literally, it's a tangible representation of the vision you have for yourself. Between all the journaling, meditation and gratitude, some ideas of what that vision looks and feels like should have come up to the surface. Your vision board is a way for you to visualize that life of success you desire in a tangible way, day after day.

You can make one by hand — think #ThrowBackThursday magazine cutouts on a bulletin board — or you can make one digitally on Pinterest. What matters is that no one else does it for you, that you select the images related to the dreams you have, and that the vision board excites you every time you see it. It can represent your vision for a particular area of your life (like your career or your relationships) or your whole life in general. And you can update it regularly as you reach each of the milestones you've manifested.

If you're feeling empowered to create your own vision board, here's how you can get started:

1 - Envision your ideal life

Now that you've started journaling and meditating regularly, start incorporating questions to determine what you want your ideal life to look like. This could be your values, your career goals, the family and relationships you want to have, your health, your dream house, the way you spend your free time, and so on and so forth. The more specific you are in your answers, the better.

Imagine yourself on a rocking chair on the front porch of your house after you've retired. You're staring gratefully at the sunset as you reflect on the amazing life you've led. What did you experience? What are you proud of? What kind of legacy do you have? How do those in your life speak about you to others? By answering these questions, you'll have a sense of your ideal life vision, meaning you can work backward to know what needs to happen for you to see it come true.

Everyone's idea of a dream life will look different depending on what your priorities and goals are. But try these ten key areas to get you started:

- You
- Self-care/ spiritual well-being
- Physical health
- Partner / Romance
- Family
- Finances
- Friends
- Career
- Giving back/impact
- Travel/hobbies/adventure

The important thing is to customize this list according to what works best for you. You'll want to dedicate some time to this; I recommend waking up early on a Saturday or Sunday morning without any distractions and letting yourself free-write in your journal or doodle on a whiteboard in your house while you ponder these questions. Then, write all your answers as vision statements in the present tense.

For example, instead of writing "I will become debt-free. I want to become financially independent." write "I am debt-free. I am financially independent." Because fantasizing this future isn't enough; it's more important to create a clear, compelling picture in our mind's eye so our brains can get busy trying to make that ideal life a reality.

2 - Write your specific future in three years' time

If imagining your ideal life in some far-off, distant future is challenging for you, try to determine how you want your life to look in three years' time.

When I was starting my business, I used the Vivid Vision exercise from Cameron Herold's book, Double Double. Even though it's geared towards business owners, it's worth trying to replicate that same level of clarity for the aspects of your life you want to improve in three years. We tend to overestimate what we're capable of doing in a year and grossly underestimate what we can do in three.

Go through the same life areas you've prioritized for yourself in the exercise above and write each of your vision statements for yourself with a three-year timeframe. So instead of saying, "I will lose weight. I will run a marathon." write something like "I am lean, fit and strong. I'm able to run the New York City Marathon."

3 - Choose your images

Once you have your vision statements for the different aspects of your life you want to prioritize, start collecting your images. You can source these visuals old-school from newspapers and magazine cut-outs, from inspiring quotes you saw online, from your Pinterest board — wherever you'd like.

Each image you choose will represent one (or more) of the vision statements you've written down. So, if one of your goals is to travel more, maybe you choose an image of a suitcase or an oceanside view of an exotic destination you've always wanted to see. Or if an aspect of your dream life is to volunteer or donate more to charity, you might choose an image of the Kiva logo or the building site for Habitats for Humanity.

4 - Pin the images on your vision board

When you sit down to create your vision board, I recommend finding a quiet space where no one will interrupt you. Set out all your supplies and let your creativity flow. Maybe you light some candles. Maybe you put on your favorite music. Maybe you meditate or set an intention before you begin. Honor the process and thank yourself for taking this valuable time out to create the life you really want to lead.

Then start creating your vision board in the way that feels right to you. There is no right way to arrange or place the images. It's your vision board so arrange the visuals you've chosen any way you'd like. Use glue, pins or tape, photos or cut-outs. Most importantly, have fun with it!

5 - Display your vision board where you can see it every day

Once you've made your vision board, it's important to place it somewhere you can see it — maybe at your desk or on your refrigerator. You don't need to stare at it 24/7 but do keep it somewhere you will come across it every day. Stop to look at it when you pass it and imagine the feeling of excitement when the ideal vision of your life starts coming true.

6 - Update your vision board

As you manifest (I know, I know, I just eye-rolled at myself) and reach your goals, be sure to add images to your vision board regularly.

7 - Love yourself and the life you're creating

Every day that you choose to create a life of success on your terms is another day you should love yourself for doing so. Remember that you're worthy of the ideal life you desire as you progress towards it.

So love yourself for the person you are and for who you are on your way to becoming.

SECTION 3

REWRITE

LEARN TO TRUST YOURSELF

"Insecurity is the lack of trust in your abilities and worth. When you enter into a secured state of consciousness, everything that helped boost your confidence will return."

-Itohan Eghide

So, what's the point of walking you through all these practices?

To help you learn to love and trust yourself. To help you listen to your inner wisdom, to reduce your stress in the face of uncertainty, to make it easier for you to make decisions, and to have the clarity you need to create a successful life that's truly on your terms.

We learn early on that to do things "right" we have to please others. We've become conditioned to seek their approval instead of trusting our own ability to guide ourselves. Maybe you struggle to make decisions because you've been conditioned to fear you'll make the wrong choice. Or you might be prone to criticizing your own decisions after you make them.

Too many of us suffer from self-doubt. We are paralyzed by indecision, our constant desire for approval, our perfectionism, and our fear of failure. Sometimes we lose trust in ourselves after we make a mistake or after someone criticizes us. Not only does self-trust become buried beneath the belief that everyone else knows better than we do, but it also becomes weakened by our constant desire to receive external validation. We become stuck in an endless feedback loop that makes us feel less worthy than we are.

The only way to break out of that loop is to turn inward and develop self-trust. Building trust in yourself boosts your decision-making skills and self-confidence. It creates a healthy, internal GPS system that depends less on what (we think) others expect of us and helps us stand firm in what we want, what's important to us, and how we want to proceed through the world with the time that we have.

When I set out to write this book, I didn't want to create an arbitrary, formulaic process for you to follow. How can I when each and every one of us is so different? When all our paths are so unique? But as I've spoken to friends, professionals, fellow entrepreneurs, and my own clients over the years, one thing became clear:

We can't show up as the fullest versions of ourselves if we don't learn to love, understand, and accept ourselves as we are.

So, my advice to you?

Try out these practices. You don't have to do all five at once but think of them as tools in your kit to come back to and use whenever you need them.

It could be meditating for five minutes each day for a month and seeing how you feel. It could be writing in a gratitude journal. It could be recording and listening to your affirmations daily on your morning commute. It could be getting up an hour earlier each day to light a candle, stare at your vision board, and remind yourself of what you truly want out of life. It could be as simple as not looking at your phone first thing in the morning and deciding to journal instead.

When you decide to commit to one of these practices and make it a habit for yourself, I suggest trying it out for at least 30 days. Accept your choice once you've made it. Ask your partner, sister or friend to join you or simply hold you accountable. And if you want to go deeper, try layering on another practice for the next 30 days or swap it out for another.

Don't overthink it — just do what feels like the next right thing for you.

The path of learning to trust yourself will require time, patience, and commitment. But I promise you, directing your attention from what's outside of you to what's inside will make all the difference.

And when you do find yourself feeling wobbly or slipping back into self-doubt (which is totally normal when you're experiencing growth or change!), you can come back to these next few chapters for a quick dose of love and encouragement from me.

NOT EVERYTHING YOU DO WILL HAVE A PURPOSE — THAT'S OK

As we covered in Chapter nine, you don't need to figure out your life's purpose today.

Purpose is not about some shiny end goal. It's ever-expanding. It's a journey that takes you deeper and deeper into what lights you up.

Stop putting so much pressure on yourself to find "the one thing you're meant to do."

How can you know your purpose when you're constantly growing? Your perspective in five, ten years — even just six months — is going to be so different from where you are today.

Purpose is not something outside of you to seek. It's turning inward to align with your truest, highest self. There's no need to strive for it, reach for it. So, what should you do?

Do what feels like the next right thing. Follow the breadcrumbs towards what feels light, what gets you fired up or just makes your heart tingle. Do you feel excitement? Do you feel joy? Then create more space in your life for whatever that is, whether it's speaking, sculpting, traveling, volunteering or simply creating. Your inner voice will give you clues to take you down the road, guiding you closer or telling you when you've strayed.

If you find yourself feeling anxious or suffocated… let it go. Even if you've made a commitment, even if it feels scary to leave it. The logical part of you will fight and say, "But I've already put so much effort in! I can't just walk away!" But the most intuitive part of you is sending you a sign to tell you to shift gears because you're straying away from what you're meant to do.

Accept that not everything you do will have a purpose other than to teach you what it is you don't want.

If it feels heavy, let it go. If it feels light, create more space to let it in.

Then follow the breadcrumbs to do what feels like the next right thing.

Keep going.

You've got this.

NOT EVERYTHING YOU DO HAS TO BE PERFECT — THAT'S OK

Done > perfect.

Did you finally decided to publish a blog post, but chickened out because your draft still needed "tweaking"? Were you feeling good about your latest piece of a lettering project, but worried that people will comment on it being "not good enough"? Did you work yourself up to submit your video to a film festival, but kept finding things to tweak in what was supposed to be the "final" edit?

Perfectionism is just another form of procrastination.

It lives and breathes and feeds on your fear of making mistakes. When you second-guess yourself, you take fewer risks or you hide in the shadows because you're afraid of negative responses.

Rather than stopping yourself from pursuing an opportunity or putting something out there because you're terrified of it being ripped apart — put out more imperfect things into the world.

We forget that people enjoy messy and imperfect. We forget they don't zoom in and see all the flaws up close like we do. We forget that where we are is exactly where we should be, and that progress is more important than perfection. We forget that what we do and create can just be for the pure joy of it, without the worry of rejection.

You're not your pain or your past. You are only what you decide to do today. So embrace the "now" instead of worrying about the million worst possibilities "later" will bring.

Whether you're a perfectionist prepping for an interview for your dream job, taking up a brand new hobby, revisiting an old childhood dream of becoming an artist, or a creative who's hiding your work in the shadows of your comfort zone... you have two choices.

Either start and simply enjoy the process or take that thing you've been tinkering with until it's "perfect" and just put it out there. And take the outcome for what is, knowing you tried your best with what you have.

We try so hard to "get it right" when we should be celebrating the baby steps that move us forward. Working toward our goals and being willing to put ourselves out there are accomplishments within themselves.

Give yourself a well-deserved pat on the back for trying, making progress and for coming as far as you have.

Keep going.

You've got this.

NOT EVERYTHING YOU DO WILL BE SUCCESSFUL — THAT'S OK

Have you ever read a description for a job and thought you're a "failure" because you only meet one or two of the requirements? Have you ever thought of pitching yourself for an opportunity but held yourself back because you thought you didn't look "perfect" on paper?

It sets off a whole domino effect, a downward spiral into an abyss of negative thoughts...

- I'll never make it as a professional photographer — everyone is already so much better and further along than I am!
- Who cares if I got a near-perfect GPA in college? I don't have any practical skills so no employer will ever want to hire me.
- I'd love to be featured in my dream publication, but I don't have that six-figure success story. They'll definitely say no, so why would I bother trying?

You have natural strengths and weaknesses — we all do. You're not going to be successful at everything you try which is 100% OK.

So stop worrying about what you're bad at. Play to your strengths instead of chasing "perfect" in every aspect of your life. Start focusing on what you're naturally good at and what you love to do.

Start by developing a talent you already have. Think about that thing you adored as a kid that brought you to your happy place. Take up that musical instrument again or sign up for voice lessons. Put your tennis, kickball or basketball skills to use by joining an intramural sports team. Head to a crafts store, buy a blank canvas, and dust off your old oil paints.

Or pick something you love (even if you think you'll be terrible at it) and join a local class. Try your hands (feet!) at that Argentine tango you've been putting off. Get pretentious AF and learn about wine and cheese pairings. Hop on a yoga mat even if you struggle to touch your toes. Maybe you'll be a total prodigy. Maybe you'll find it's not your cup of tea. Maybe you'll get better over time. And even if you don't, you'll walk away with a cool new experience and a greater appreciation for people who have a skill set different from your own.

Whatever you decide, approach it with gratitude and grace. Be humble. Enjoy the process. Let go of the outcome and be OK with the fact that you won't "get it right" instantly.

There's always a new skill to learn, a new tool to master. There's always one more thing that can be done. But the good news is, you don't have to win at everything. In fact, you probably can't. No one can do everything well.

Instead, choose what you love to do and the process of learning — and focus on that.

Remember: everything you try, every step you take is a step closer to the clarity you need to build a successful life on your terms.

Keep going.

You've got this.

YOU WON'T FOLLOW THROUGH WITH EVERYTHING YOU DO — THAT'S OK

A couple of years ago, I was invited to walk the Camino de Santiago with a friend in the days leading up to her birthday. Our plan was to walk 285 kilometers (177 miles) from Avilés to Santiago de Compostela across the north of Spain.

It's a distance that most walk at a leisurely pace, staying at whichever albergue or pilgrim hostel is closest when you decide to stop for the day. Taking post-lunch siestas under the shade of a tree overlooking a river. Or taking off your boots to dip your toes into the ocean as you watch the sunrise. It takes anywhere from three to five weeks to trek that distance and we planned to do it in 16 days.

We called it quits after day three.

It was much more challenging than either of us had anticipated. Our bodies couldn't handle the frenetic pace. My left knee and hip started aching so badly I had to stop walking earlier each day. My Camino buddy pushed through the pain and ended up needing an operation on her ACL when she flew back home to the US.

But neither of us saw it as defeat.

We still ended up celebrating her birthday in Santiago de Compostela with my husband and her family just like we'd planned. The road we each took to get there changed but the destination stayed the same.

It was such a poignant reminder about the nature of life itself.

We won't finish or follow through with everything we do. Maybe the timing isn't right. Maybe other obligations call us away. Maybe we realize the thing we thought we so desperately wanted isn't what we expected at all. So we walk away.

And you know what? That's absolutely OK.

I know I'll walk the Camino again someday and that it'll be there waiting, just as it has been for wayfaring pilgrims for thousands of years. I know I'll feel the exhilaration of finishing, whether it's months or years from now. I see it as a pause rather than me giving up. And even if I never walk it again — that's fine by me, too.

You don't have to finish everything you start. You don't have to follow through on something solely because you think, "I've already put all this time, effort, and energy in." If that's the only thing that's making you stick around, then definitely leave it. You and you alone will know if you tried your absolute best.

If it feels heavy, move on. Accept the lesson. Communicate honestly with whoever is involved in your decision. Then walk away to create space for something new, somewhere you can bring the lessons you've learned into this next phase of your life.

Keep going.

You've got this.

DECIDE: COMMIT TO YOURSELF & FOLLOW THROUGH

"It is our choices… that show what we truly are, far more than our abilities."

-J.K. Rowling

It's no secret that I'm a massive Harry Potter fan. I've got my official Gryffindor scarf and cardigan and a mug that I drink from regularly with "I solemnly swear I am up to no good" emblazoned on the side. (Heck, as soon as Javi and I decided we were going to Scotland for our next trip, I bought our seats to ride the Jacobite train *before* our plane tickets.)

Wizarding world aside, what this Muggle admires most about the Harry Potter series is Rowling herself. She went from being a jobless single mother living off unemployment benefits to one of the best-selling authors of all time. To me, it's a story of triumph in the face of overwhelming odds.

But it didn't happen overnight. She faced depression, a failed marriage, and rejection upon rejection. She worked hard at her craft before anyone noticed her, even when she was, in her own words, "the biggest failure I knew". Despite numerous setbacks, she found solace in doing what she loved, strengthening herself against rejection and, ultimately, putting her work out into the world to make the massive impact it had.

When you make a decision to create a life on your terms, you're fully committing to move toward your goal, regardless of the demons, detractors, and Dementors that are flung onto your path. And stuff will definitely be flung your way to stop you from moving forward — otherwise we'd all be living fabulous lives we love.

The moment it gets hard or you risk looking like a complete fool, remember your decision. Remember your commitment to yourself. Remember what you are creating and why you are in this. Remember that you made the decision to move toward the life you want to create. Hold fast to that commitment. Fall flat on your face, ask for help when you need it, then get back up on your feet and follow through.

In order to change your life, your faith (in yourself and in miracles) must be greater than your fear. However easy or rough the process is, you must be willing to make a mess, clean it up, and then not stop until you get wherever you've decided to go.

When I visited the Harry Potter studios in London, I couldn't help but geek out. I squealed with glee as I walked down Diagon Alley, peered into the Gryffindor common room, and marveled at the details of the Dark Forest. It was midway through the tour as I stood outside the doors of 12 Grimmauld Place that I realized… this entire, colorful world that's become a phenomenon the world over… all started with ONE.

All too often when we're caught up in the day to day of our business, looking ahead to others' success with a mixture of admiration and envy…we forget that everything, like J.K. Rowling's success with Harry Potter, started with one.

One person.

One idea.

One decision.

One foot in front of the other.

One commitment to keep going.

Until one day, that one idea impacted enough people.

Your story, as messy and imperfect as it seems now, has the capacity to change hundreds if not millions of lives. And it all starts with one person: you.

So love yourself, friend. Love who you are and who you are becoming.

You can do anything you wholeheartedly decide to do.

DESIRE: WHAT YOU WANT ALREADY EXISTS... TRUST THE PROCESS

"Surrender to what is. Say 'yes' to life and see how life suddenly starts working for you rather than against you."

-Eckhart Tolle

I want to commend you for taking the time to step back, zoom out, and consciously decide how you want to move forward to create a life on your terms. Because I know you're a dreamer who's also ready to do the work.

But I also want to include a caveat here. I've experienced burnout from solely focusing on the end goal, without having a purpose behind why I wanted it. I've slipped back into depression when I charged so fearlessly at something, forcing things around me to bend with all my might so that I could achieve it, only to find that I pushed away the outcome I desired. It's a hard lesson to learn and one that I'm continuing to learn as a recovering-Type-A-perfectionist-overthinker-overachiever.

My greatest achievements in life and business didn't just come from hard work alone. They came from me opening my tight-fisted grip and being receptive to surprises that were far more meaningful than anything I could have dreamt up for myself.

I hit my highest monthly income goal when I cut back on my working hours. I landed a dream interview with Thrive Global when an editor found me and asked me to share my story. If I'd held too fast to a goal, wishing and willing it to look the exact way I'd envisioned in my head, I wouldn't have had the open heart to receive unexpected outcomes.

So even though you're all pumped up, psyched to get this journey started, and prepped to take things head-on...

Remember to surrender.

Remember that this new beginning, this unbecoming, this next chapter — it's uncharted territory for you. You're not going to have all the answers right away. Don't rush to find out the how or the what. Just take comfort in knowing that the why, the intention behind your decision to create a life you truly desire, is enough for now.

Remember that when we want something so badly and work tirelessly to get it, gripping the goal so tightly... we're forcing instead of allowing something to come in naturally.

There comes a point where we have to hand over our decision to the unseen forces around us. We have to allow instead of force, to release instead of karate chop our way through. We have to trust that if we have clarity on our life's purpose and move forward with grace and gratitude, the opportunities that are most aligned with who we are will hurtle towards us. Sometimes your new reality will look exactly like you imagined. Sometimes it will be completely different (and way better!).

To surrender fully and completely, you've gotta have faith in the Universe, God, the Magical Motherlode, the Source Energy or whatever you refer to it as. You need to have absolute clarity on what you desire and trust that it's already on its way to you.

Decide that what you desire is yours to receive. Regularly check in with your inner voice, journaling, meditating, affirming, envisioning, and giving thanks for what's already in your life. Choose what feels like the next right step toward what you desire. As you take heart-centered, purpose-driven action toward creating the life of your dreams, be open to whatever comes your way.

Most of all, love yourself for who you are and who you are becoming.

DO: REWRITE YOUR STORY

"Life is simple. Everything happens for you, not to you. Everything happens at exactly the right moment, neither too soon nor too late. You don't have to like it... it's just easier if you do."

-Byron Katie

If you were a passenger in a speeding car heading towards a cliff, would you sit back and do nothing? Or would you take the wheel?

This book is your invitation to take back the wheel and steer your life in the direction you choose, on the road you decide to take, toward the future you desire. And that starts with you accepting this truth:

Your life is happening *for* you. Not *to* you.

Regardless of what you've lived up to this point, your story can be rewritten. You get to let go of the old stories that have held you back, kept you down, and made you feel less than that incredible human being you are. Either you hold onto those stories or you set yourself free to enjoy a life of your making.

Whatever you decide to do — pursue comedy, learn hip hop, study French, start a business, fall in love, lose weight, direct movies, raise five kids, travel the world, open an orphanage, save the trees, fight against climate change, quit your job, run for office — believe that it's possible. Then commit to making it so.

You get to reshape the narrative. So give yourself permission to do so, regardless of what anyone around you thinks is possible for you right now. And in the process, fall back in love with yourself for the person you are and who you are consciously deciding to become.

You are capable.

You are powerful.

You are worthy.

You are enough.

You are loved.

To Day One of creating a successful life that's truly on your own terms.

ABOUT THE AUTHOR

The Professional Bio...

Kay Fabella is a brand and visibility strategist who helps underrepresented entrepreneurs 400x their audience and impact. Stories = visibility = diversity = equality — and it's Kay's mission to lead a movement for WOC business owners who are ready to step into the spotlight and create a ripple effect in the online space. Her book *Rewrite Your Story* is part memoir, part practical guide on how to recover, reclaim, and rewrite your life story after burnout as she's done with her own business.

Kay graduated in three years with a bachelor's degree in International Relations and Economics, and after college worked in international NGOs, educational institutions, start-ups, and multinational corporations before opening her business in 2014.

Today she operates as The Story Finder, Kay's bilingual English/Spanish personal brand that reached an audience in 27 countries in less than three years. She leveraged her experience as a Filipina-American expat based in Spain to help companies grow their visibility through the power of storytelling. Kay has been featured in Fast Company, Thrive Global, Huffington Post and in the Spanish-language newspaper, El País.

A Los Angeles native, Kay now lives in Madrid, Spain, with her husband, Javi, and their two cats. The official language in their house is Spanglish.

If/when you run into me on the street...

...first off, please don't charge at me. I'm an HSP introvert who doesn't react well to loud noises and I will put my musical lungs to use to burst your eardrums out of sheer terror. So, you know, wave at me nicely until I see you?

If you do engage in conversation, here are 15 topics we can jam on:

- Harry Potter
- Me falling out of yoga inversions
- Identity, diversity, and belonging
- Sriracha (hot sauce in my bag, swag)
- Bourbon, craft beer, and mezcal
- Brené Brown
- Transcendental meditation
- David Attenborough's narration
- Jane the Virgin
- Oprah's Super Soul Sunday podcast
- Star Trek
- Intersectional feminism
- Ali Wong
- TED Talks
- Marvel comics

...and life abroad with my Spanish husband and cats, por supuesto.

I'm an INFJ and a Leo who doesn't really like red or being the center of attention (or horoscopes). I have an unofficial master's degree in waist-up dressing #WorkFromHomeLife, and a Ph.D. in Know My Shit. I snort-laugh hard when something's funny and I cry at good commercials.

My passion in life is helping people who feel unseen to find, share, and stand in their stories.

Loved this book? Finally found the courage to rewrite your story? I'd love to know! Please email me at hello@kayfabella.com or subscribe to my blog at kayfabella.com.

For more helpful resources to help you rewrite your own story, head to **rewriteyourstorybook.com.**

Thank you for letting me share my story with you.

All my best,

Kay

ACKNOWLEDGMENTS

To my husband, Javi, who is the rock-solid foundation upon which I continue to grow, spread my wings, and thrive. Thank you for loving me as I am, every day. Your constant support inspired me to find my voice and help others do the same. Te quiero morski.

To my biz besties, Emma, Chloe, Janneke, Alessia, Ariana, Cher, and, of course, Jessica and Heather. And gratitude for my Madrid family, Alondra, Rosie, Maria, Elisha, and Lauren. You've all held space for me as I've found my story, held me accountable even when it was hard, and encouraged me every step of the way. I'm grateful for each and every one of you.

I also wish to extend my heartfelt thanks to my pre-release crew: Kara Fabella, Craig Smith, Emma Perols, El Edwards, Emily Cox, Anibal Santos, Ryan Day, and Ricardo Londoño.

And, of course, to the countless clients, family members, and friends who've cheered me on as I've worked to get my story out there. You've all added to my journey and I wouldn't be here without you.

Made in the USA
Monee, IL
30 July 2020